Turn your knowing into growing.

There's more to the Word than meets the mind, says Robert E. Coleman. There's a dimension of understanding that reaches into your heart and actually changes your life. If you — or someone you know—desire to experience that dimension, this book can help. The author's helpful introductions clarify the importance of each lesson for new and mature believers alike; insights into the value of regular study habits and Scripture memorization will help you develop daily sensitivity to God's truth; and this self-discovery method gives you the opportunity to apply that truth in your own life. Whether your Christian walk consists of decades or days, these lessons can show you the exciting difference between knowing the Bible and actively *Growing in the Word*.

BY Robert E. Coleman

Growing in the Word

Bible Lessons For Growing Christians

ROBERT E. COLEMAN

SPIRE BOOKS

Fleming H. Revell Company
Old Tappan, New Jersey

Scripture references in this book, unless otherwise noted, are from the King James Version of the Bible.

Permission to quote from the following books is gratefully acknowledged.

From *Christian Perfection* by François de Salignac de La Mothe Fenelon, edited by Charles F. Whiston, translated by Mildred Whitney Stillman. Copyright 1947 by Harper & Row, Publishers, Inc. Reprinted by permission of the publisher.

From *Bees in Amber* by John Oxenham. © Copyright 1959. Reprinted by permission of Desmond Dunkerley.

From *Love Song*, A New Translation of Augustine's Confessions (Harper & Row, 1971), by permission of the translator, Sherwood Eliot Wirt.

From "How To Be Filled With the Spirit" in *Revival in Our Time* by Billy Graham. Copyright by The Billy Graham Evangelistic Association. Used by permission.

Much of the material in this volume is taken from the series of Bible studies: *Established by the Word*, copyright © 1959, 1960, 1962, 1964, 1969, 1975 by Robert E. Coleman; *Life in the Living Word*, copyright © 1961, 1962, 1965, 1967, 1968, 1975 by Robert E. Coleman; *The Spirit and the Word*, copyright © 1965, 1969, 1975 by Robert E. Coleman.

ISBN 0-8007-8448-0

"... Shine as lights in the world, holding fast the Word of life." (Philippians 2:15, 16 RSV)

CONTENTS

INTRODUCTION

The Christian life is revealed in the Word. The Word is the life. Yet it is not a doctrine or a creed that lives, but a Person——the living Word of God Himself, Jesus Christ. He is the Word "made flesh" (John 1:14) by which the eternal God is personally made known and His life experienced. When you receive His Word into your heart, then you receive His life. That is what Christianity is.

But lest your experience be unfounded on fact, or become subject to the changing whims of public opinion, God has seen to it that His Word is preserved from error by having it committed to writing. The result is the Bible——the divinely inspired history of God's redemptive work among men, which was finally and perfectly disclosed in the Person of Jesus Christ. The Word written in the Book is the visible authority for the Word written in your heart. Since both are the work of the same Spirit, there can be no contradiction between what the Bible says and what you experience.

As such, the Bible is not only the *record* of what God has done to disclose Himself and His salvation, but it is also the *means* by which that revelation is realized in your life. While differing in form, it is nevertheless part of God's redeeming truth, and where properly understood and faithfully obeyed, it will invariably bring you to Him who is "the way, the truth, and the life" (John 14:6). That is the whole purpose of Scripture. It is "written, that ye might believe that Jesus is the Christ, the Son of God; and that believing ye might have life through his name" (John 20:31).

For this reason, if you would know more about Christ, you must know more about the Bible. It is the instrument of the Holy Spirit by which your mind is illumined (2 Timothy 3:16; John 5:39), your heart convicted (Hebrews 4:12), and your faith kindled (Romans 10:8, 17; 1 John 5:13). And through that faith, it is the Word that regenerates your heart (1 Peter 1:23; 2 Peter 1:4), sanctifies your life (John 15:3; 17:17; Ephesians 5:26), feeds your soul (1 Peter 2:2), builds you up (Acts 20:32), and gives you joy, peace, and security forevermore (Psalm 119; 1 John 1:4; Acts 15:31; Romans 15:14).

It is easy to see that your Christian life is rooted and established in the Book. Yet, all too many Christians rest their faith on nothing more than personal experience. The result is that some are confused and uncertain in their witness, while many others are ignorant of the extensive blessings which are theirs in Christ. With them the problem is not so much in believing the Word, nor even in having a knowledge of Christ, but in actually knowing what the Bible says about their salvation.

That is why this book is written. It seeks to encourage growing disciples to discover the meaning of redemption in the only perfectly reliable source. First lessons deal with basic truths in your new Christian experience. As the study progresses, more attention is given to doctrine, particularly in relation to present possessions in Christ. Finally you are led to work through some of the deeper aspects of the Holy Spirit's sanctifying ministry, and the promise of victorious living.

Since so much of your growth in grace and knowledge rests upon a discipline of devotion, there are also some suggestions for keeping a daily quiet time, as well as a few tips for continuing Bible study and Scripture memory.

The brief compass of the book naturally requires considerable selection in the topics chosen. Many things have had to be passed over, or mentioned only briefly. But an attempt has been made to come to grips with matters which have a very practical bearing upon your life and witness.

Let these lessons help you in your personal time with the Word every day. Also, try to develop in doing them a skill of Bible study on your own. Although the methods followed are very elementary, the disciplines required can teach you many deeper principles of learning. However, you will have to apply yourself diligently. "Rightly dividing the word of truth" is the task of a "workman" and you will want to do your best to be "approved unto God" (2 Timothy 2:15).

Certainly this will be a delightful exercise to your soul. The more you live in "the word of life" (Philippians 2:16), the more wonderful your life becomes. Similarly the more you know about Christ, the more you can understand what is written. He is the Master Key to all truth. In Him are hid "all the treasures of wisdom and knowledge" (Colossians 2:3). And as you apply to your life what you learn, the living Christ will become more meaningful and blessed in your experience day by day.

And this is the record, that God hath given to us eternal life, and this life is in his Son.

1 John 5:11

HOW TO USE THIS BOOK

In Your Personal Study

1. Use this book along with your Bible. Any translation will do.
2. Read carefully the introduction to each lesson.
3. Study a few questions every day. Be regular. Develop a habit of Bible study.
4. After reading the question, look up the Scripture reference. If the first reference is not clear, try the second one given in parentheses.
5. Pray that God will lead you to find the truth in each Bible verse.
6. Think on the verse long enough to understand clearly what it *says*, then determine what it *means* to you.
7. Write a brief answer to the question in your own words. Be yourself. Try not to copy the Bible answer word for word.
8. Write your personal application at the end of each lesson. This will help you to make the meaning your own.
9. Memorize the Scripture verses in connection with each lesson. You will thus be enabled continually to meditate upon the Word of God.
10. Any unanswered questions in your mind take to your pastor or counselor. This experienced adviser can then review your progress and give you further instruction.

In Group Study

This book may be used as a study guide in a small group. In this case, the procedure is the same as that outlined for the individual, except that the completed lessons are discussed among the participants. Thus the group itself assumes the supportive role of the pastor or counselor in reviewing the work and in making additional assignments. A good way to conduct the meeting is to have some group members read their answers to key questions, with opportunity given for explanation of the views expressed. The personal applications especially will lead to insights during discussion. Problems which arise can be shared in the fellowship as each person seeks in love to build up the other, "and so fulfill the law of Christ" (Galatians 6:2). Concerns of the group can be focused in prayer, with thanksgiving to God.

Holy Bible, Book divine,
Precious treasure, thou art mine;
Mine to tell me whence I came,
Mine to teach me what I am;
Mine to guide me where I go,
Mine to tell me what to do,
Mine to show the way of love,
Mine to counsel and reprove;
Mine to tell of joys to come
In my Heav'nly Father's home.
O thou holy Book divine,
Precious treasure, thou art mine.

                                   —JOHN BURTON

Whatever keeps me from the Bible—is my enemy, however harmless it may appear to be. Whatever engages my attention—when I should be meditating on God and things eternal—does injury to my soul.

Let the cares of life crowd out the Scriptures from my mind and I have suffered loss where I can least afford it. Let me accept anything else instead of the Scriptures—and I have been cheated and robbed to my eternal confusion.

——A. W. TOZER

Within that awful volume lies
The mystery of mysteries!
Happiest they of human race,
To whom God has given grace
To read, to fear, to hope, to pray,
To lift the latch and force the way;
And better had they ne'er been born,
Who read to doubt, or read to scorn.

——SIR WALTER SCOTT
The Monastery

I surrendered my will to the living God revealed in Scripture. I knelt before the open Bible, and said: "Lord, many things in this Book I do not understand. But Thou hast said, 'The just shall live by faith.' All I have received from Thee, I have taken by faith. Here and now, by faith, I accept the Bible as Thy word. I take it all. I take it without reservations. Where there are things I cannot understand, I will reserve judgment until I receive more light. If this pleases Thee, give me authority as I proclaim Thy word, and through that authority convict me of sin and turn sinners to the Saviour."

——BILLY GRAHAM

Part One

Essential Facts For New Christians

At thirty after examining the philosophies and religions of the world, I said that nothing is better than the Gospel of Christ. At forty, when burdens pressed heavily and the years seemed to hasten, I said: Nothing is as good as the Gospel. At fifty, when there were empty chairs in the home and the mound builders had done their service, I said: Nothing is to be compared with the Gospel. At sixty, when my second sight saw through the illusions and vanities of earthly things, I said that there is nothing but the Gospel. And then at seventy, amid the many limitations and privations, I sang:

"Should all the forms which men devise
Attack my faith with treacherous art,
I'd call them vanity and lies,
And bind the Gospel to my heart."

—a story told by Robert G. Lee

The world finds its consummation not in finding itself but in finding its Master; not in coming to its true self but in meeting its true Lord and Savior; not in overcoming but in being overcome. We are more than conquerors: we are redeemed. That is the Word of the Christian Gospel.

—P. T. FORSYTH

A father who wanted to teach his son about God's love, took him to the top of a high hill and pointed northward over Scotland, southward over England, eastward over the ocean, westward over hill and valley, and then sweeping his arm around the whole circling horizon, he said, "Johnny, my boy, God's love is as big as all that." "Why, father," the boy replied with sparkling eyes, "then we must be right in the middle of it."

I love you, Lord, not doubtingly, but with absolute certainty. Your Word beat upon my heart until I fell in *love with you. . . .*

And what do I love when I love you? Not physical beauty, or the grandeur of our existence in time, or the radiance of light that pleases the eye, or the sweet melody of old familiar songs, or the fragrance of flowers and ointments and spices, or the taste of manna or honey, or the arms we like to use to clasp each other. None of these do I love when I love my God. They are the kind of light and sound and odor and food and love that affect the senses of my inner man.

There is another dimension of life in which my soul reflects a light that space itself cannot contain. It hears melodies that never fade with time. It inhales lovely scents that are not blown away by the wind. It eats without diminishing or consuming the supply. It never gets separated from the embrace of God and never gets tired of it. That is what I love when I love my God.

. . . I came to love you late, O Beauty so ancient and so new; I came to love you late. You were within me and I was outside, where I rushed about wildly searching for you like some monster loose in your beautiful world. You were with me but I was not with you. You called me, you shouted to me, you broke past my deafness. You bathed me in your light, you wrapped me in your splendor, you sent my blindness reeling. You gave out such a delightful fragrance, and I drew it in and came breathing hard after you. I tasted, and it made me hunger and thirst; you touched me, and I burned to know your peace.

All my hopes are in your great mercy and nowhere else. So give what you command, and command what you will. It is your order that we should practice self-control; and man who insists on loving something besides you does not really love you as he should, unless he loves it because of you. O Love that always burns and is never extinguished! O Love that is my God, set me afire!

——SAINT AUGUSTINE
Confessions

THE GOOD NEWS

   You heard the good news——the best news that anyone has ever heard——the news that "God so loved the world, that he gave his only begotten Son, that whosoever believeth in him should not perish, but have everlasting life" (John 3:16). You may have heard it many times before, but this time it was different——you believed it.

   You believed God. That's why the Gospel makes sense now. This truth is hidden to those who do not believe (2 Corinthians 4:3, 4). The very first principle of knowledge is to believe that God is true to His Word. "Then faith cometh by hearing, and hearing by the word of God" (Romans 10:17).

   The truth at first was not pleasant to face. You saw yourself for what you truly were——a sinner. You had rebelled against God, and had come under the just penalty of death and hell. You knew that you were guilty. There was no use denying it any longer. You were lost, "having no hope, and without God in the world" (Ephesians 2:12).

   Yet you believed the good news that God still loved you. God "so loved" you that He was willing to take upon Himself the judgment of His own law of righteousness by offering His Son to die in your stead. Jesus took your place, "the just for the unjust" that He might bring you to God (1 Peter 3:18).

   Jesus paid it all. He bore in His own blameless body the

shame, the suffering, and the utter separation from the Father caused by your sin. It was a terrible price, but it was the only way that God could cancel out your iniquity and still maintain His justice. There on the cross God made full satisfaction for the sins of the whole world. The atonement was finished. Everything was done that needed to be done to provide a salvation from all sin for all men.

You knew that you were unworthy of such love. But God did not give you what you deserved; He gave you grace—unmerited love. It was simply a "gift of God: not of works, lest any man should boast" (Ephesians 2:8, 9).

All that you could do was to take God at His Word and accept His gift. And God asked nothing more. There were no strings attached to His condition for salvation: "Believe on the Lord Jesus Christ, and thou shalt be saved" (Acts 16:31). Yet to believe, you had to confess and forsake all sin, and commit all that you are to Jesus in childlike trust.

This is the simple plan of salvation. It's all that a sinner needs to know to be saved. You heard it. You believed it. You came to Jesus, and in repentance and faith, asked Him to save you. You may not have known how to pray, but you could say in your own way this much:

"I am a sinner. I need a Savior. I believe that Jesus died for my sins. I forsake my sins, and by faith in God's Word, I now accept Jesus Christ as my Savior and Lord. By God's grace, I will serve and obey Him all my life."

This is not the prayer of a righteous man wanting justice, but the earnest plea of a sinner seeking mercy. And where it is sincerely prayed, God always answers for the sake of His Son. "For whosoever shall call upon the name of the Lord shall be saved" (Romans 10:13).

Find It For Yourself

1. Why is the Gospel such good news? Luke 2:10, 11

2. Why do people need to hear the Gospel? Romans 3:23 (Romans 5:12)

3. Sin has many aspects. There are sins of commission (doing what is wrong), sins of omission (not doing what is right), and unbelief in God's Word. To be specific, what is sin in respect to the law of God? 1 John 3:4 (Mark 7:21, 22)

4. What is sin in respect to lost opportunity and privilege? James 4:17 (Matthew 23:23)

5. What is the expression of sin in respect to the Gospel of Christ? John 16:9 (John 3:19)

6. What is the consequence of sin? Romans 6:23 (Genesis 2:17)

7. The penalty of sin is death, so how could God uphold

His law and still let sinners go free? 1 Peter 3:18 (2 Corinthians 5:21; Isaiah 53:6)

_____

_____

_____

8. What happened then to your sin when God permitted His Just Son to die for the unjust on the cross? 1 Peter 2:24 (Galatians 1:4; 1 John 3:5)

_____

_____

9. Why did God who was perfect in Himself ever let His Son go through such humiliation and suffering to redeem a rebellious people? John 3:16 (Romans 5:8)

_____

10. How many people does God's love embrace? John 3:16 (Romans 10:13)

_____

11. What must you do to be saved? John 3:16 (Acts 16:31)

_____

12. Name some ways in which you express saving faith, that is, taking God at His Word and acting accordingly. John 1:12 (Matthew 7:13; Revelation 3:20; Romans 10:10)

_____

_____

13. What must you do about your sin when you believe
    the Gospel? Mark 1:15 (Luke 13:3)

_____

14. What does it mean to repent? Isaiah 55:7 (Luke
    15:21)

_____

15. What does Jesus promise to all who sincerely come
    to Him? John 6:37 (Matthew 11:28)

_____

16. When does Jesus invite you to come and be saved? 2
    Corinthians 6:2 (Isaiah 55:6)

_____

17. Why do you not have to wait until you are better or
    have done more good works to be saved? Ephesians
    2:8, 9 (Titus 2:11)

_____

_____

18. In a sentence, what then does grace mean? Titus 3:5
    (Romans 5:15; 11:6)

_____

_____

---

*For I am not ashamed of the gospel of Christ: for it is
the power of God unto salvation to every one that
believeth; to the Jew first, and also to the Greek.*
Romans 1:16

Make Your Own Application

Write out your experience of faith in the Gospel of Christ, telling why it is such good news to you, and how you have turned from sin unto God and accepted His grace.

_____
_____
_____
_____
_____
_____
_____
_____
_____
_____
_____
_____

Memorize *John 3:16 and Romans 1:16*

I believe in one Lord Jesus Christ, the only-begotten Son of God, begotten of His Father before all worlds, God of God, Light of Light, very God of very God, begotten, not made, being of one substance with the Father, by whom all things were made; Who, for us men, and for our salvation, came down from heaven, and was incarnate by the Holy Ghost of the Virgin Mary, and was made man; and was crucified also for us under Pontius Pilate. He suffered and was buried; and the third day He rose again, according to the Scriptures; and ascended into heaven, and sitteth on the right hand of the Father. And He shall come again with glory to judge both the quick and the dead; Whose kingdom shall have no end.

——FROM THE NICENE CREED

If you knew that there was One greater than yourself, who knows you better than you can know yourself, and loves you better than you can love self, who can make you all you ought to be . . . if He were a youthful God who would understand you because He is ever young, yet with the wealth of the ages and eternities so that you would be always learning and never exhausting the store; One who gathered into Himself all great and good things and causes, blending in His beauty all the enduring color of life, who could turn your dreams into visions, and make real the things you hoped were true; and if that One had ever done one unmistakable thing to prove, even at the price of blood——His own blood——that you could come to Him . . . would you not fall at His feet with the treasure of your years, your powers, service and love? And is there not One such, and does He not call you from His cross to His cross? Is there any excuse of divided churches, inconsistent Christians or intellectual difficulty that can withstand His steady inviting gaze?

——Author unknown

Christianity is . . . distinctively a religion of Redemption—a great Divine economy for the recovery of men from the guilt and power of sin—from a state of estrangement and hostility to God—to a state of holiness and blessedness in the favor of God, and of fitness for the attainment of their true destination. . . . We may, therefore, set aside at once as alien to the true Christian view, or at least as inadequate and defective, all such representations of Christianity as see in its Founder only a great religious teacher and preacher of righteousness; or a great religious and social reformer; or one whose main business it was to inoculate men with a new "enthusiasm for humanity"; or a teacher with a new ethical secret to impart to mankind; or even such representations as see in Him only a new spiritual Head of humanity, whose work it is to complete the old creation, and lift the race to a higher platform of spiritual attainment, or help it a stage further onwards to the goal of perfection. Christ is all this, but He is infinitely more. God's end in His creation indeed stands, as also His purpose to realize it; but, under the conditions in which humanity exists, that end can only be realized through a Redemption, and it is this Redemption which Christ pre-eminently came into the world to effect.

—JAMES ORR

Not only do we know God by Jesus Christ alone, but we know ourselves only by Jesus Christ. We know life and death only through Jesus Christ. Apart from Jesus Christ, we do not know what is our life, nor our death, nor God, nor ourselves.

Thus without the Scripture, which has Jesus Christ alone for its object, we know nothing, and see only darkness and confusion in the nature of God, and in our own nature.

—BLAISE PASCAL

Lesson 2

CHRIST IN YOU

Jesus Christ is a personal Savior. He does not give you a mere philosophy of life or a code of ethics. He gives you Himself. The Christian life is not a creed or a dogma. It is the living fellowship with a real Person—the Son of God who loved you and gave Himself for you.

For your sake, He who could speak worlds into being accepted for a time human flesh, became a servant, was tempted in all ways as you are, suffered, died, was buried, and rose again from the grave. When by faith you identified yourself with Him, you not only died with Christ on the Cross, but you also rose with Christ in the power of His resurrection.

Do not underestimate what has happened. Your life is made new. "If any man be in Christ, he is a new creature: old things are passed away; behold, all things are become new" (2 Corinthians 5:17). God does not just put new clothes on your back; He puts a new man in your clothes.

His life is imparted to you through the Holy Spirit. The transforming power of the Spirit indwelling your heart by faith is so real that it is likened to "being born again" (1 Peter 1:23). This does not mean that God destroys your human nature and abilities. Quite the contrary. He takes your natural powers and bends them to perform their true created purpose. Christ thus enables you to fulfill your destiny as a person created in the image of God.

The life you now live is not your own. You belong to Christ. He has redeemed you by His own blood. All that you are and all that you hope to be you owe to Him. He is your righteousness, your peace, your joy—"Christ in you, the hope of glory" (Colossians 1:27).

He that hath the Son hath life; and he that hath not the Son of God hath not life.

1 John 5:12

But as many as received him, to them gave he power to become the sons of God, even to them that believe on his name.

John 1:12

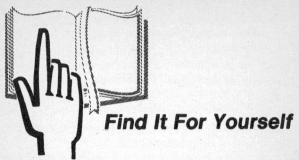

Find It For Yourself

1. What was the great reason for the Bible to be written? John 20:31

_____

_____

2. Why does everything depend upon what you do with Jesus? John 14:6 (Acts 4:12)

_____

_____

3. Who is this Person around whom all the events of redemption revolve? Not to leave this question in doubt, God the Father said: Matthew 3:17 (Matthew 17:5)

_____

The angels said: Luke 1:32 (Luke 2:11)

_____

The apostles said: John 6:69 (John 20:28)

_____

People that believed said: John 4:42 (John 11:27)

_____

4. Why then did Jesus, who was One with God, almighty in power, ever come to earth? Luke 19:10 (1 Timothy 1:15)

_____

5. How did Jesus so completely identify Himself with your human circumstances? Philippians 2:7, 8 (Romans 5:19)

6. What are the essential events in the life of Christ which you have participated in by faith? 1 Corinthians 15:3, 4

7. What happened when you believed that Christ died on the cross for you? Romans 6:6 (Colossians 3:3)

8. What happened when you believed that Christ rose from the grave for you? 2 Timothy 2:11 (Romans 8:11)

9. Having ascended back into heaven, what does Christ continue to do for you now? Hebrews 7:25 (Romans 8:34)

10. What does Jesus plan to do for you someday? John 14:3 (Acts 1:11)

11. What did you become in relation to God by virtue of your faith in Jesus Christ? John 1:12 (1 John 3:2)

12. How does this new sonship of God come about? John 1:13 (John 3:3, 5, 7)

13. What is the teaching instrument through which the new birth is known? 1 Peter 1:23 (2 Peter 1:4)

_____

14. Who is the Agent of God effecting the new birth? Romans 8:9 (Titus 3:5)

_____

15. How do you recognize the presence of the Holy Spirit within? 1 Corinthians 12:3 (John 16:14)

_____

16. How close is Christ related to you through the indwelling Holy Spirit? John 14:20 (John 15:5)

_____

17. What does the Spirit give to you that makes your nature different? John 6:63 (2 Corinthians 3:6)

_____

18. What then happens to your old nature when you come to Christ? 2 Corinthians 5:17 (Galatians 6:15)

_____

19. To summarize, what two types of people are there in the world? 1 John 5:11, 12 (John 3:36)

_____

_____

_____

Make Your Own Application

Tell why Jesus Christ is worthy of your trust and how your life has found fulfillment in Him, using as a reference Galatians 2:20 and Philippians 1:21.

_____
_____
_____
_____
_____
_____
_____
_____
_____
_____
_____

Memorize John 1:12 and 1 John 5:12

In Christ Jesus we work no longer for life, but from life. Our high endeavor is not to shape our actual life in the flesh into conformity to an ideal life that is set before us in Him. It is rather to reduce our true life now hid in Christ to an actual life in ourself. And so the summons of the Gospel is not that we behold what is possible for us in Christ, and reach forth to it; but rather we behold what is accomplished for us in Christ, and appropriate it and live in it.

——A. J. GORDON

We need an experience of Christ in which we think everything about the Christ and not about the experience.

——P. T. FORSYTH

*Someone asked Luther, "Do you feel
    That you have been forgiven?"
He answered, "No, but I'm as sure
    As there's a God in heaven.
For feelings come, and feelings go,
    And feelings are deceiving;
My warrant is the Word of God,
    Naught else is worth believing.*

*"Though all my heart should feel condemned
    For want of one sweet token,
There is one, greater than my heart,
    Whose Word cannot be broken.
I'll trust in His unchanging love,
    Till soul and body sever;
For though all else shall pass away,
    His Word shall stand, forever."*

——Author Unknown

C. H. Spurgeon was talking to a farmer who had a weather vane on his barn that contained the words,

"God is love." He asked the farmer: "What do you mean by that? Do you think God's love is change-able—that it veers about as the arrow turns in the wind?"

"Oh, no!" answered the farmer. "I mean that which-ever way the wind blows, God is still love."

Where shall my wondering soul begin?
    How shall I all to heaven aspire?
A slave redeemed from death and sin,
    A brand plucked from eternal fire,
How shall I equal triumphs raise,
Or sing my great Deliverer's praise?

O how shall I the goodness tell
    Father, which thou to me hast showed?
That I, a child of wrath and hell,
    I should be called a child of God,
Should know, should feel my sins forgiven,
Blest with this antepast of heaven!

—CHARLES WESLEY

The story is told of an old Scottish woman who was dying, and in accordance with the custom, the pastor came by to see if she really was a true believer.

"Do you still trust in Christ," he asked.

"Ah, yes I do," she replied. "He is my only hope in life and in death."

The minister then asked, "Do you believe that He will take you to heaven?"

"Yes," she answered, "I know He will."

"But suppose that He doesn't?"

The old saint thought for a moment, then replied, "Ah, God may do what He wills, but if He doesn't take me to heaven, He will lose more than me. Though I will lose my soul, God will lose His honor, for He has said that those who trust in His Son shall never perish."

—Original author unknown

Lesson 3

NO DOUBT ABOUT IT

Salvation is real. You can know it. God does not intend for you to be in doubt about this most essential thing in life. He has given you the Bible, not only that you might believe on His Son, but also "that ye may know that ye have eternal life" (1 John 5:13).

Moreover, the same Spirit that inspired the writing of the Scriptures will testify to the reality of the Word received by faith unto your own heart. "It is the Spirit that beareth witness, because the Spirit is truth" (1 John 5:6). He will vouch with your spirit that you are a child of God (Romans 8:16).

Understand though what this assurance is. It is not necessarily a feeling of emotion, although emotion may accompany it. Salvation is something you know, not because you feel it, but because you are certain that Jesus died for your sins and rose again from the grave for your justification. These are facts which are true whether you feel like shouting or crying. Your assurance rests upon the faithfulness of God, that when you meet the conditions of His Word, He always fulfills His promises.

That which you feel within is the realization that your sins are forgiven and that you are free from condemnation. There is a resulting sense of inner peace, abiding joy, and confidence in the future. You do not know what the future holds, but you know God loves you, and He holds your future.

This is your assurance. The sin which separated you and God is nailed to the Cross. You are reconciled. God is no stranger to you any longer. He is your Father. You are His adopted child. The Bible is your authority. The Holy Spirit is your inner witness. Your own sense of peace agrees. That's enough to settle any doubt.

> *These things have I written unto you that believe on the name of the Son of God; that ye may know that ye have eternal life, and that ye may believe on the name of the Son of God.*
>
> 1 John 5:13

> *Verily, verily, I say unto you, He that heareth my word, and believeth on him that sent me, hath everlasting life, and shall not come into condemnation; but is passed from death unto life.*
>
> John 5:24

Find It For Yourself

1. What is the written guarantee of eternal life? 1 John 5:13

_____

2. How does the Bible accomplish its purpose in you, that is, how must you receive the Word to know that you are born of God? 1 John 5:1, 10 (John 5:24)

_____

3. When you meet this basic condition of faith, not in yourself, but in Christ, what is there about the nature of God that assures you of salvation? Hebrews 10:23 (2 Thessalonians 3:3)

_____

4. How do you know in experience that the doctrines you believe are of God? John 7:17 (John 8:31, 32)

_____

5. How does God confirm the truthfulness of what you believe directly to your heart and mind? 1 John 4:13, 5:6 (1 Corinthians 2:12)

_____

6. What especially is the relationship with God, resulting from your faith in Christ, to which the Holy Spirit bears witness? Romans 8:16 (Galatians 4:6)

_____

7. Believing God's Word, what do you know that He has done with your sins? Colossians 2:13 (1 John 2:12)

_____

8. How does this sense of complete forgiveness manifest itself in your consciousness? Romans 8:1 (John 3:18)

_____

9. What does the absence of any condemnation of sins do for your assurance of salvation? 1 John 3:21

_____

10. How does your trust in Jesus affect your anxiety about the future and the fear of death? John 14:1, 2, 3 (2 Timothy 1:7)

_____

_____

11. Loving God and His calling, what wonderful assurance do you have about the way things happen to you? Romans 8:28 (2 Corinthians 4:17)

_____

_____

12. If your life on this earth were suddenly ended by death or the second coming of Christ, what assurance do you have? 2 Corinthians 5:1 (1 John 3:2)

_____

13. How might you sum up the way one feels now who has his or her faith firmly fixed in God? Romans 5:1 (Romans 15:13)

_____

_____

14. What is the way a Christian feels toward others which confirms the assurance of salvation? 1 John 3:14 (1 John 3:18, 19)

_____

_____

15. A Christian will love God and all human beings, but how is this love expressed? 1 John 5:2 (1 Jn. 2:3, 5)

_____

_____

16. What is the confidence which you have so long as you walk obediently in all the light of God's Word that you understand? 1 John 1:7 (1 John 2:17, 24, 25)

_____

_____

17. How does the assurance of salvation express itself in your public testimony? 2 Timothy 1:12 (Acts 2:36; 1 John 5:20)

_____

_____

_____

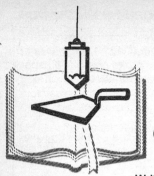

Make Your Own Application

Write out why you know that your salvation is real, and tell what you know is true in regard to your past, present, and future in the light of John 5:24.

_____
_____
_____
_____
_____
_____
_____
_____
_____
_____
_____
_____

Memorize 1 John 5:13 and John 5:24

A man is just as strong as the thing he commits himself to. If I venture out upon the broad ocean in a paper box, as soon as the water has penetrated the box it goes to pieces and I am lost. But if I commit myself to a steamer, neither the storms nor the waves can injure me.

If a man commits himself to the flesh, he will be weak as the flesh; but if he commits himself to God he will stand until God goes down.

——SAM JONES

As soon as you perceive yourself tempted follow the example of children when they see a wolf or a bear in the country; for they immediately run into the arms of their father or mother, or at least they call out to them for help. Look not the temptation in the face, but look only on our Lord; for if you look at the temptation, especially while it is strong, it may shake your courage. Divert your thoughts to some good and pious reflections, for when good thoughts occupy your heart they will drive away every temptation and suggestion.

It is a very good sign that the enemy keeps knocking and storming at the gate, for it shows that he has not what he wants. If he had he would not make any more noise, but enter in and quietly remain there.

——FRANCIS OF SALES

If you have a doubtful issue in your life, something with a question mark after it, put it to this fourfold test. The Test of Expediency (1 Corinthians 6:12): It may even be good, but is it good for me to do? The Test of Enslavement (1 Corinthians 6:12 again): Does it make me its slave? The Test of Edification (1 Corinthians 10:23): Does it build me up? The Test of Example (1 Corinthians 3): Does it offend the weaker brother? If your problem clears these four hurdles, it should no longer be a problem.

——VANCE HAVNER

A weary little boy climbed to a seat beside his "new father" on an old wagon. He had just left the train that had brought him the long, aching miles from a little home which had seen much sorrow these last days.

Mother had been quietly taken from the arms of her only little lad and from the hushed home to be placed gently beside the father in the little cemetery on the slopes outside the village.

Friends had explained so inadequately that "Daddy and Mother had gone to heaven" and that the boy was to have a "grand train ride to a new daddy."

Well, here he was, sitting high on the wagon and looking into the kindly eyes of his adopted parent as they ride toward the boy's new home.

The child sat so quietly that the new father, watching tenderly, noted that the lad was preoccupied and frequently slipped his hand into his coat.

"Why do you look off in the distance, son, and move your hand so strangely within your coat? I'm going to try to fill your daddy's place."

The boy came from his thoughts and began to explain: "You know, Mister-er, Daddy, before they took Mother away, I cut a piece from her dress and hid it in my coat, and now when I'm lonely I like to slip my hand in my coat, and feel of Mother's dress, 'cause then it most seems as if Mother were right close by me."

Say, have you ever been weary of this old world and lonesome for heaven? Then slip your hand over the Book and hold its truths close to your heart, and you will say, "It seems as if my Lord is close by."

—told by Mervin E. Rosell

In your temptations run to the promises; they be our Lord's branches hanging over the water, that our Lord's poor, half-drowned children may take a grip of them; if you let that grip go you will go to the bottom.

—SAMUEL RUTHERFORD

Lesson 4

OVERCOMING TEMPTATION

When you gave yourself to Christ, you became an overcomer. "For whatsoever is born of God overcometh the world: and this is the victory that overcometh the world, even our faith. Who is he that overcometh the world, but he that believeth that Jesus is the Son of God?" (1 John 5:4, 5)

However, the victory is won through conquest. You might as well face it now: the devil will fight every advance you make, and sometimes your faith will be sorely tried. You must "fight the good fight of faith" to win (1 Timothy 6:12). It would be tragic to assume that you will not be tempted, or that you could not fall back into sin.

But your God is bigger than any adversary which you may face. He will not let you be tempted more than you can withstand. Through His strength, you can be more than a conqueror. In fact, your trials can be turned into opportunities for real spiritual growth and blessing if you will just mind God.

If through your failing you give way to a temptation, immediately confess it to God. You have an "advocate with the Father, Jesus Christ the righteous" (1 John 2:1). Renew your commitment to Him, turn your back on the sin, and He will forgive you. Doing anything which you know displeases God will break your fellowship with Him, and thereby cause you to lose your confidence.

Beginning with Christ was wonderful, but overcoming with Him day by day is even better. You get to see His faithfulness demonstrated continually. No matter what comes, His grace is sufficient to handle any problem. He is able to supply all your needs "according to his riches in glory" (Philippians 4:19). So "be strong in the Lord, and in the power of his might" (Ephesians 6:10).

There hath no temptation taken you but such as is common to man: but God is faithful, who will not suffer you to be tempted above that ye are able; but will with the temptation also make a way to escape, that ye may be able to bear it.

1 Corinthians 10:13

If we confess our sins, he is faithful and just to forgive us our sins, and to cleanse us from all unrighteousness.

1 John 1:9

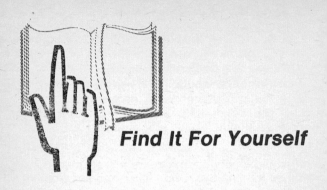

Find It For Yourself

1. Who is it that overcomes the world? 1 John 5:5

---

2. How do you have this power to overcome? 1 John 4:4 (John 16:33; Philippians 4:13)

---

3. What does God promise to do according to His power in Christ Jesus? Philippians 4:19 (Ephesians 3:20)

---

4. Why is the Christian life beset with conflict and struggle? 1 Peter 5:8 (Ephesians 6:12)

---

5. What kind of a Person is this Devil that seeks to capture the souls of men? John 8:44 (2 Corinthians 11:14)

---

6. In addition to the deceitful attacks of Satan, how do temptations arise? James 1:13, 14 (Mark 7:21–23)

---

7. God is never the Author of temptation, but He does permit His people to be tested. In this sense, what good can come out of temptations that one overcomes? James 1:2-4, 12 (Zechariah 13:9)

_____

_____

8. What can you be sure of in respect to every temptation that comes your way? 1 Corinthians 10:13

_____

_____

_____

9. What must you do when temptations arise? James 4:7 (1 Timothy 6:11)

10. Even though there may be strong intentions never to sin, what must you be doing to strengthen your resistance to temptation since the human flesh is weak? Matthew 26:41 (Matthew 6:13)

11. What may you be sure of when you bring your problems before the Lord in prayer? Hebrews 2:17, 18 (Hebrews 4:14-16)

_____

_____

12. How did Jesus resist the Devil when he was being tempted? Matthew 4:4, 7, 10 (Ephesians 6:17)

_____

13. It being true that Jesus found great strength in knowing the promises of God during His temptation, how can you draw upon these same resources when you need them? Psalms 119:11 (Romans 10:8)

_____

_____

14. What is the only thing that can ever separate you from God? Isaiah 59:2 (Joshua 7:11, 12)

_____

15. Since sin separates from God, what should be your attitude toward it? Romans 6:12 (1 John 3:9)

_____

16. It is clear that a Christian is expected to overcome the world through the power of Christ in him, but what can you do if sin is allowed to break your fellowship with God? 1 John 1:9 (1 John 2:1)

_____

17. What does confession mean in addition to asking God to forgive the sin? Proverbs 28:13 (Hebrews 12:1)

_____

_____

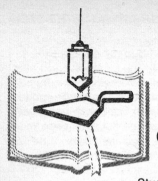

Make Your Own Application

Study Romans 8:35–39 and write out the things which God says cannot separate you from the love of God in Christ Jesus. Tell why you have victory now over your present circumstances.

_____
_____
_____
_____
_____
_____
_____
_____
_____
_____
_____

Memorize *1 Corinthians 10:13 and 1 John 1:9*

I pluck an acorn and hold it to my ear, and this is what it says to me: "By and by the birds will come and nest in me. By and by I will furnish shade for the cattle. By and by I will provide warmth for the home. By and by I will be shelter from the storm to those who have gone under the roof. By and by I will be the strong ribs of a great vessel, and the tempest will beat against me in vain, while I carry men across the great sea."

"Oh, foolish little acorn, wilt thou be all this?" I ask. And the acorn answers, "Yes, God and I."

I look into the faces of a company of children, and I hear a whisper, saying: "By and by I will be a great blessing to many. By and by other lives will come and find rest and home in me. By and by the weary will sit in the shadow of my strength. By and by I will sit as comforter in a home of sorrow. By and by I will shine in the full radiancy of the beauty of Christ, and be glorified with my Redeemer."

"You, frail, powerless little one?" I ask. And the answer is, "Yes, Christ and I."

——LYMAN ABBOTT

"We never become truly spiritual by sitting down and wishing to become so. You must undertake something so great that you cannot accomplish it unaided."

——PHILLIPS BROOKS

"God loves with a great love the man whose heart is bursting with a passion for the impossible."

——WILLIAM BOOTH

As a man who has borrowed a great sum feels his joy for having the money alloyed by the obligation to restore it, and by the anxiety he is in as to whether he shall be able to pay it at the time appointed, so he who is humble, the more gifts he receives from God the more he acknowledges himself a debtor and under a stricter obligation to serve Him; and, thinking that his gratitude and services do not answer, as they ought, the greatness of the favors and benefits he has received, he believes at the same time that anyone but himself would have made a better use of them. It is this which makes the servants of God more humble than others; for they know that God will call them to account not only for the sins they commit, but also for the benefits they receive. "Unto whomsoever much is given, of him shall be much required" (Luke 12:48).

But why is God so pleased to exalt the humble, and to confer upon them so many favors? It is because all the good He does them returns to Himself. For they who are humble appropriate to themselves nothing of what they receive; they restore it all to God, and, acknowledging that there is nothing great but the power of God alone, ascribe to Him the glory and honor of all.

——ALPHONSUS RODRIGUEZ

I heard the voice of Jesus say.
    "I am this dark world's Light;
Look unto Me, thy morn shall rise,
    And all thy day be bright."
I looked to Jesus, and I found
    In Him my Star, my Sun;
And in that Light of life I'll walk,
    Till travelling days are done.

——HORATIUS BONAR

Little self-denials, little honesties, little passing words of sympathy, little nameless acts of kindness, little silent victories over favorite temptations——these are the silent threads of gold which, when woven together, gleam out so brightly in the pattern of life that God approves.

——F. W. FARRAR

Lesson 5

GROWING IN GRACE

The Christian life is always growing up "unto a perfect man, unto the measure of the stature of the fulness of Christ" (Ephesians 4:13). No matter what you have already attained in the grace of God, there is more beyond. To stop growing is to stop living.

This continual process of growth will not always be easy. There will be times of real struggle and suffering which you must pass through. You will doubtless learn many things about your life now which will need to be brought into conformity to the obedience of Christ as your understanding of God's will enlarges.

You will come to see, for example, that you need to be cleansed from any root of bitterness remaining in you. Experience will show your need of continual infilling with the Holy Spirit in order to serve God effectively. Old habits may have to be broken, new disciplines formed, and many attitudes changed. There are many things that need to be added to your faith——virtues which reflect the character of Him whom you love and praise.

The secret of this ever-expanding life in the fullness of God is simply to walk in all the light which He gives. Obey without question everything which He tells you to do. Follow Jesus all the way. He is Lord of your life. This will mean a daily denial of your own rights in loving submission to His sovereignty.

God has great things for you. He will lead you on as fast as you can go. Never get discouraged if the way seems slow. He intends someday "to present you faultless before the presence of his glory with exceeding joy" (Jude 24). So keep pressing on to "the mark for the prize of the high calling of God in Christ Jesus" (Philippians 3:14).

But if we walk in the light, as he is in the light, we have fellowship one with another, and the blood of Jesus Christ his Son cleanseth us from all sin.

1 John 1:7

He that hath my commandments, and keepeth them, he it is that loveth me: and he that loveth me shall be loved of my Father, and I will love him, and will manifest myself to him.

John 14:21

Find It For Yourself

1. It is recognized that every new Christian starts out as a spiritual babe in Christ, but when you grow up, what are you expected to become as a man? Ephesians 4:13–15

2. In order to grow to maturity in Christ, what food must you have? 1 Peter 2:2 (Jeremiah 15:16)

3. As a child gradually takes a stronger diet of the Word, growing in the knowledge of God, what normally is he expected to do with his childish ways? 1 Corinthians 13:11 (Hebrews 5:14)

4. What pitiful condition is soon evident when a young Christian does not digest more meat of the Word and progressively develop into manhood? Hebrews 5:12, 13 (1 Corinthians 3:1, 2)

5. Realizing that there comes a time when a Christian looks pathetic still sucking a baby bottle, what should you do after the more elemental doctrines of Christ are mastered? Hebrews 6:1 (Matthew 5:48)

6. What about your character should you always be perfecting? 2 Corinthians 7:1 (Hebrews 12:14)

_____

7. Why is holiness of life so necessary to you? 1 Peter 1:15, 16 (Matthew 5:8; 1 Thessalonians 4:7)

_____

8. Holiness is likeness to God, and He wants you to be like Him, but how are you made pure and holy in His sight? Hebrews 13:12 (Ephesians 5:26; Hebrews 10:10)

_____

9. How do you appropriate holiness and every other benefit of the atonement of Christ? Acts 15:9 (Acts 26:18)

_____

10. How does this faith come to you which sanctifies and cleanses your heart? John 17:17 (John 15:3)

_____

11. What especially should you be increasing in as you perfect your faith in Christ? 1 Thessalonians 3:12 (Colossians 3:12–14)

_____

12. Love is the greatest expression of holiness, but what are some other virtues in your Christian life which should be cultivated? 2 Peter 1:5–7 (Galatians 5:22, 23)

_____

_____

_____

_____

13. What should you endeavor to think about during the day? Colossians 3:1, 2 (Philippians 2:5; 2 Corinthians 10:5)

_____

_____

_____

_____

14. In the light of Christ's love for you, what is your reasonable service to Him? Romans 12:1 (2 Corinthians 4:11)

_____

_____

15. What does it mean to make a full surrender to Jesus Christ? Matthew 16:24 (Philippians 3:8)

_____

_____

16. How is your loving sacrifice to Christ expressed in terms of daily conduct? John 14:21, 23 (Matthew 16:24)

_____

17. As you strive toward your goal, keeping your eyes upon Christ, what progressively happens to you by the Spirit? 2 Corinthians 3:18 (Colossians 3:10)

_____

_____

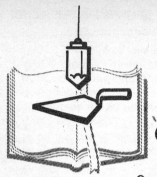

Make Your Own Application

One of the best descriptions of what the ethical behavior of a Christian should be is in 1 Corinthians 13:4-7. List the characteristic ways this love should be manifested in your life. It will be helpful to consult several different Bible translations of this passage.

_____
_____
_____
_____
_____
_____
_____
_____
_____
_____
_____
_____

Memorize 1 John 1:7 and John 14:21

I want to know one thing, the way to heaven . . . God Himself has condescended to teach the way . . . He hath written it down in a book. O give me that book: At any price give me the book of God! I have it: here is knowledge enough for me. Let me be "a man of one book" (translated from Latin) . . . I sit down alone: only God is here. In His presence I open, I read His book; for this end, to find the way to heaven . . . Does anything appear dark and intricate? I lift up my heart to the Father of lights . . . I then search after and consider parallel passages . . . I meditate thereon . . . If any doubt still remains, I consult those who are experienced in the things of God: and then the writings whereby, being dead, they yet speak. And what I learn, that I teach.

—JOHN WESLEY

Tell of his wondrous faithfulness,
    And sound His power abroad;
Sing the sweet promise of His grace,
    And our performing God.

Engraved as in eternal brass
    The mighty promise shines;
Nor can the powers of darkness rase
    Those everlasting lines.

His very word of grace is strong
    As that which built the skies:
The voice that rolls the stars along
    Speaks all the promises.

—ISAAC WATTS

The story is told of a shabby old gentleman who every day at twelve o'clock would enter the church, stay a few minutes, then leave. One day the caretaker accosted him. "Look here, my friend, what are you up to, going into the church every day?"

"I go to pray," replied the old man politely.

"Now come," the cautious caretaker said, *"you don't stay long enough to pray."*

"True enough. I cannot pray a long prayer, but every day I just comes and says, 'Jesus, it's Jim.' Then I waits a minute, then comes away."

One day Jim was knocked down crossing the street and was laid up in the hospital with a broken leg. The ward where he lay, notorious for the grumbling of the patients, began to take on a joyful air.

"What has come over all of you?" asked the nurse.

"It's old Jim," they replied. *"He's always cheerful, never complains, although in pain."*

The nurse walked over to Jim's bed where he lay with an angelic look on his smiling face. *"Well, Jim, these men say you are the cause for the change in this ward. They say you are always happy."*

"Aye, that I am, nurse. I can't help it. You see, nurse, it's my visitor. He makes me happy."

"Visitor?" The nurse was indeed puzzled for she had never noticed any visitor by Jim's bed. *"When does your visitor come?"*

"Every day," replied Jim with the light in his eyes growing brighter. *"Yup, every day at twelve o'clock He comes and stands at the foot of my bed. I see Him there, and He smiles at me and says, 'Jim, it's Jesus.' "*

——Author Unknown

"Prayer is the working of a will that is free, within a will that is sovereign."

——A. J. GORDON

If you can beat the devil in the matter of regular daily prayer, you can beat him anywhere. If he can beat you there, he can possibly beat you anywhere.

——PAUL RADER

Lesson 6

BASIC DISCIPLINE

Christian experience forms spiritual habits in your personal life which nourish and deepen your devotion to God. As such, these disciplines are absolutely necessary if you are to grow up in Christ.

The Guidebook for your development, as has already been noted, is the divinely inspired and interpreted Bible. It is the means by which God speaks to your faith. As a child desirous of the Father's will, you should learn as much of His Word as you can. Read it carefully, study it systematically, memorize it diligently, meditate upon it continuously and practice it faithfully.

You commune with God through prayer. It is the air which your spirit breathes. You cannot live without it. Pray in the morning when you get up, and again before going to bed at night. Always give thanks to God before every meal. And sometime during the day, if possible, have prayer with your family.

In addition, the habit of investing a longer period of time alone with God every day would be of immeasurable benefit to your spiritual life. During this quiet time, you can more leisurely search the Scriptures and meditate upon the purposes of God for your life.

You also need to faithfully support a church where the pure Word of God is preached, and the sacraments duly administered. It is part of the Body of Christ. Give it your most devoted prayers, your presence, your gifts and your service. You cannot develop as you should without this fellowship with others, seeking with them the power of godliness, watching over one another in love, and endeavoring together to work out your salvation.

If ye abide in me, and my words abide in you, ye shall ask what ye will, and it shall be done unto you.

John 15:7

Thy word have I hid in mine heart, that I might not sin against thee.

Psalms 119:11

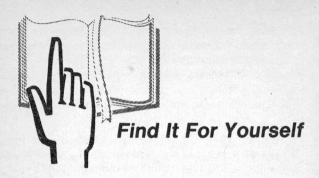

Find It For Yourself

1. What is more necessary than food for you to live?
   Job 23:12

   _____

2. From a practical standpoint, why must you have the
   Word of God to live every day? Psalms 119:105, 130
   (2 Peter 1:19)

   _____

   _____

3. Why is the Bible an infallible Guide in all matters of
   faith and practice? 2 Timothy 3:16 (2 Peter 1:20, 21;
   1 Corinthians 2:13)

   _____

   _____

4. It is assuring to know that God so inspired the chosen
   men who wrote the Scriptures that they were
   guarded against any error in their selection of words
   to express the truth which He wanted revealed, but
   how does God guide you in interpreting these words?
   John 16:13 (1 Corinthians 2:12)

   _____

   _____

5. Since the Holy Spirit interprets the Scriptures which He inspired, what is a good thing to do when you open the Bible? Psalms 119:18, 27 (James 1:5)

6. You must ask God to help you understand the Bible, but what must you do on your part to really get the meat of the Word? 2 Timothy 2:15 (Acts 17:11)

7. What should you do with the Word of God in your mind day and night? Joshua 1:8 (Psalms 1:2)

8. What does Jesus promise those who abide in His Word? John 15:7 (Luke 11:9, 10)

9. How does the Holy Spirit help you when you pray in Christ? Romans 8:26, 27 (1 Corinthians 2:10)

10. What can block the channel of prayer in your life? Psalms 66:18 (1 John 3:21, 22)

11. Why are some prayers of good men unanswered? James 4:3 (1 John 5:14, 15)

12. How does faith affect your prayer to God? Matthew 21:22 (Mark 11:24)

13. In what attitude must prayer and supplications be offered? Philippians 4:6 (Ephesians 5:20)

_____

14. What are some things for which to pray? Psalms 139:23, 24

_____

Ephesians 3:19

_____

John 17:20, 21

_____

15. How does Jesus regard the value of prayer in small groups? Matthew 18:19

_____

16. What must Christians be careful not to neglect? Hebrews 10:25 (Deuteronomy 12:5)

_____

17. How are members of the church to regard one another? Galatians 6:2 (James 5:16; 1 Corinthians 12:12)

_____

18. What is a good habit to form in your support of the church? 1 Corinthians 16:2 (2 Corinthians 9:7)

_____

Make Your Own Application

Jesus taught His disciples to pray after the manner recorded in Matthew 6:9–13 (Luke 11:2–4). Outline in your own words the seven things asked for in the prayer. Note especially how the worship of God and submission to His will precedes your own concerns.

_____

_____

_____

_____

_____

_____

_____

_____

_____

_____

_____

Memorize John 15:7 and Psalms 119:11

If the Gospel is just that way of understanding religion which is meaningful for me, which helps me and comforts me, then I have no right to interfere with others who have their own versions of it, their own ways to such peace and security as men can hope for. But the Gospel is the truth, and therefore it is true for all men. It is the unveiling of the face of Him who made all things, from whom every man comes, and to whom every man goes. It is the revealing of the meaning of human history, of the origin and destiny of mankind. Jesus is not only my Savior; He is the Lord of all things, the cause and cornerstone of the universe. If I believe that, then to bear witness to that is the very stuff of existence.

—LESSLIE NEWBIGIN

"I do not believe any man ever yet genuinely, humbly, thoroughly gave himself to Christ without some other finding Christ through him. I wish it might tempt some of your souls to the higher life."

—PHILLIPS BROOKS

"To be a witness is not to make propaganda, not even to shock people; it is to create a mystery. It is to live in such a way that life is inexplicable if God does not exist."

—CARDINAL SUHARD OF PARIS

The Greek word meaning "to take alive" occurs only twice in the New Testament: in Luke 5:10 and 2 Timothy 2:26. In the one case Jesus promises to enable His disciples to take men alive for the Kingdom. In the other, Paul speaks of those who have been taken alive by the devil. It is the same word in both cases, but with a different outcome! By one or the other fisher of men every soul will eventually be taken—taken alive unto death, or taken alive unto eternal life.

—CHARLES G. TRUMBULL

Christians are supposed to be the "salt of the earth." But the salt is stockpiled! The church has become a warehouse. Let it serve rather as a salt refinery, sending its product into a needy world.

——W. DAYTON ROBERTS

Jesus, and shall it ever be,
A mortal man ashamed of Thee?
Ashamed of Thee, whom angels praise,
Whose glories shine through endless days?

Ashamed of Jesus! just as soon
Let midnight be ashamed of noon;
'Tis midnight with my soul, till He,
Bright Morning Star, bid darkness flee.

Ashamed of Jesus! that dear Friend
On Whom my hopes of heaven depend!
No, when I blush, be this my shame,
That I no more revere His name.

Ashamed of Jesus! yes, I may,
When I've no guilt to wash away,
No tear to wipe, no good to crave,
No fear to quell, no soul to save.

Till then——nor is my boasting vain——
Till then I boast a Savior slain;
And O, may this my glory be,
That Christ is not ashamed of me.

——J. GRIGG

"He who does all, even the commonest things, as in God's presence, is still working for God, although he may appear to do nothing of more importance."

——FRANÇOIS FENELON

Lesson 7

SAVED TO TELL OTHERS

God has made a tremendous investment in you. He expects a return. You were chosen "that ye should go and bring forth fruit, and that your fruit should remain" (John 15:16). He not only saved you from sin; He saved you for His work. He has a job for you. You were "created in Christ Jesus unto good works" (Ephesians 2:10).

Your good deeds, of course, are not the basis of your salvation. You are saved only by the grace of God through faith. But having been redeemed, you start working for God. Now others, seeing your good works, give glory to your Father in heaven. God gets the credit, but someday you will get the reward.

God is counting on you. You are His instrument in ministering to the needs of the world. Look around for these opportunities for service. Surely there is something you can do. He will give you the strength to do His work, if you will only trust Him and let Him lead you on.

Above all God wants you to represent Him before those who do not know the Gospel. This was the supreme mission of His own Son when He came to earth, "not to be ministered unto, but to minister, and to give his life a ransom for many" (Mark 10:45). Now in the power of His Spirit He sends you out to be His witness "unto all men of what thou hast seen and heard" (Acts 22:15).

The love of Christ constrains you to this task. It is your reason for living. You are born to reproduce. What a thrill! You are a co-laborer with Christ in telling the good news of salvation to the ends of the earth and unto the end of time.

That which we have seen and heard declare we unto you, that ye also may have fellowship with us: and truly our fellowship is with the Father, and with his Son Jesus Christ.

1 John 1:3

Go ye therefore, and teach all nations, baptizing them in the name of the Father, and of the Son, and of the Holy Ghost: teaching them to observe all things whatsoever I have commanded you: and, lo, I am with you alway, even unto the end of the world.

Matthew 28:19, 20

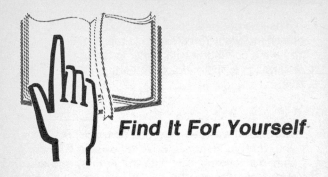

Find It For Yourself

1. Why did God choose to save you? John 15:16

_____

2. How does God feel if you do not bring forth fruit in your life? John 15:2 (Luke 13:6–9)

_____

3. It is certain that no amount of good works save you since you are saved by faith in Christ, but why are they so important? James 2:17, 18 (Titus 3:8)

_____

_____

4. How can pure religion be defined in this sense of un- selfish service? James 1:27 (Romans 13:10)

_____

_____

5. When you, in love, help others, who are you actually serving? Matthew 25:40 (John 21:16)

_____

6. How do your good works, done in the name of Christ, reflect upon God? Matthew 5:16 (1 Peter 2:12)

_____

7. What did Jesus regard as the supreme work of God? John 6:29 (John 6:40)

___

8. Since the whole work of God is summed up in Jesus Christ, what will become of those who refuse to participate by faith in His salvation? John 8:24 (John 3:18)

___

9. Moved by love for the multitudes who were lost, Jesus came into the world to save sinners. In the light of Christ's work, if you follow Him, what will you become? Matthew 4:19 (Luke 5:10)

___

10. Since God works through human personality, what does the world so desperately need today? Matthew 9:38 (Romans 10:14, 15)

___

11. Why should you be willing to do the work of Christ? 1 John 3:16 (2 Corinthians 5:14)

___

12. What are you expected to tell those you see who do not know the Savior? 1 John 1:3 (Acts 22:15)

___

13. What do you realize when a soul is converted to Christ? James 5:20 (Matthew 18:3)

___

14. How has God provided the spiritual power for you to be His witness for Christ? Acts 1:8 (Luke 24:49)

_____

15. What is the great commission which Jesus gave to His people? Matthew 28:19, 20 (Mark 16:15)

_____

_____

_____

_____

16. By whose authority do you make disciples? Matthew 28:18

_____

17. What does Jesus promise to those who obey His great commission? Matthew 28:20

_____

18. What reward has God promised to all who are faithful unto the end? 2 Timothy 4:8 (1 Peter 5:4)

_____

19. What should you do with the things that you learn from this study? 2 Timothy 2:2 (1 Peter 5:2)

_____

_____

Make Your Own Application

Reviewing the principles of the Gospel studied in Lesson 1, tell how you would explain to the lost sinner what he must do to be saved. Recall your own experience as an illustration of what you mean.

_____

_____

_____

_____

_____

_____

_____

_____

_____

_____

_____

Memorize *1 John 1:3 and Matthew 28:19, 20*

Part Two
Your Possessions In Christ

A Christian should be a striking likeness of Jesus Christ. You have read lives of Christ, beautifully and eloquently written, but the best life of Christ is His living biography, written out in the words and actions of His people. If we were what we profess to be, and what we should be, we would be pictures of Christ; yea, such striking likenesses of Him that the world would not have to hold us up by the hour together, and say, "Well, it seems somewhat of a likeness": but they would, when they once beheld us, exclaim, "He has caught the very idea of the holy Man of Nazareth, and he works it out in his life and everyday actions."

——C. H. SPURGEON

Let everything you see represent to your spirit the presence, the excellency, and the power of God. And let your conversation with the creatures lead you unto the Creator. For so shall your actions be done more frequently with an actual eye to God's presence by your often seeing Him in the glass of the creation. In the face of the sun you may see God's beauty; in the fire you may feel His heat warming; in the water, His gentleness to refresh you; He it is that comforts your spirits when you have taken cordials.

Let us remember that God is in us, and that we are in Him; we are His workmanship, let us not deface it; we are in His presence, let us not pollute it by unholy actions.

God is in every place; suppose it, therefore, to be a church. And that decency of deportment and piety of carriage which you are taught by religion or by custom, or by civility and public manners, to use in churches, the same use in all places.

——JEREMY TAYLOR

This union is, of course, not physical, but spiritual, and can be known to the one who has entered into it by the direct witness of the Spirit; but this can be known to others only by its effects and fruits in the life.

This spiritual union is mysterious yet simple, and many of our everyday relationships partially illustrate it.

Where two people have interests or purposes the same, they are to that extent one. A husband and wife, or a boy and his mother, may be separated by continents and seas, and yet be one. For six months three thousand miles of wild waves rolled between me and the woman I rejoice to call "wife," but my heart was as absolutely true to her and my confidence in her fidelity was as supreme as when we sit side by side——and we are one.

But more perfect, more tender, more holy and infinitely more self-consuming and ennobling and enduring is the union of the soul with Jesus than is any other possible relationship. It is like the union of the bay with the sea. It is the union of a nature, a commingling of spirit, an eternal marriage of heart and soul and mind.

——COMMISSIONER SAMUEL LOGAN BRENGLE

One of the great similarities between Christianity and marriage is that, for Christians, they both get better as we get older.

——JEAN A. REES

In one of the great art galleries of Europe a young man stood enrapt before a portrait done by one of the great masters. As he looked his eyes filled with tears. Another visitor to the gallery noticed him standing there and said, "Young man, what troubled you?" Still gazing at the painting, the youth replied, "I can't paint like that. I never will be able to paint like that." Then his face brightened, "But, thank God," he said, "I am a painter too."

CALLED BY HIS NAME

Do you know what your name means? Oh, yes, as far as the title given you by your parents is concerned, you know that it identifies you and your reputation as a person. Thus it can be said that a man is as good as his name. But if this is the case, consider what it means to be called a Christian—to be identified with the reputation of Jesus Christ.

Amazing as it may seem, this is exactly what happens when you are saved. In effect, the character of Christ is ascribed to you. Because He was willing in His love to make "himself of no reputation" (Philippians 2:7), and assume your name as the son of man, now you can live in the Name of the Son of God. When this fact grips you—when you actually accept His life as your own, and renounce your old life of sin, then He lets you live by His reputation.

Think of what this means. Like a bride bequeathed to her husband, you relinquish your old identity, and assume the Name of your Lord—the Name by which the worlds were made and the stars hung in place—the Name before which nations are judged and empires fall—the only "name under heaven given among men, whereby we must be saved" (Acts 4:12)—the "name . . . above every name," that at its mention "every knee should bow" and "every tongue should confess that Jesus Christ is Lord, to the glory of God the Father" (Philippians 2:10, 11).

As a person in the eyes of the world, you may not amount to much, but you can say that you have a great God and Savior. And after all, it is not who you are, or what you have done that matters. You stand before God in the virtue of who He is, and what He did to redeem your soul. Never forget it! Christ alone is your sufficiency. He is all you have, but He is all you need. "Salvation, and glory, and honour, and power" belong unto your Lord. (Revelation 19:1).

That if thou shalt confess with thy mouth the Lord Jesus, and shalt believe in thine heart that God hath raised him from the dead, thou shalt be saved.
Romans 10:9

Wherefore he is able also to save them to the uttermost that come unto God by him, seeing he ever liveth to make intercession for them.
Hebrews 7:25

Find It For Yourself

1. Where do you see life as it is meant to be? John 1:4; 14:6 (2 John 5:11)

2. When you see the Christ, whom do you actually see revealed in human form? John 14:9 (John 10:30; 12:45; Colossians 1:15)

3. How is Christ described in reference to His disclosure of God? John 1:1, 14 (1 John 1:1; 5:7)

4. How long has Christ existed? John 1:1; 8:58; 17:5 (Revelation 1:8; 22:13; Micah 5:2)

5. What did He do in the beginning to visibly demonstrate His power? John 1:3 (Colossians 1:16, 17; Hebrews 1:10)

6. Since He was before all things, and created all things, what should every creature acknowledge about Him to the glory of God? Philippians 2:11 (Acts 10:36; 1 Timothy 6:15)

7. All this speaks of the majesty of Christ, but in terms of love within the Person of God, what is the relationship which He has with the Father? Mark 1:1 (Hebrews 1:1, 2)

---

8. How did the Son of God become the son of man? Luke 1:35 (Matthew 1:20)

---

9. What was His purpose in coming into the world of human history? John 10:10 (Luke 19:10)

---

10. What did Jesus realize that He had to do in order to give you His life? Matthew 20:28 (John 10:11, 17, 18; 12:24, 32, 33)

---

11. Why do you think the shedding of blood is so prominent in Christ's mission to the world? Hebrews 9:22; 1 Peter 1:18, 19 (Isaiah 53:7; Leviticus 17:11)

---

12. By pouring out His life unto death through the shedding of His blood, what did the Lamb of God once and for all accomplish? Titus 2:14 (Revelation 1:5)

---

13. What is the great proof that God gave to the world verifying the claims of His Son? Romans 1:4 (1 Peter 1:3, 21)

_____

14. Because He lives, what can you be sure of now? John 14:19 (Hebrews 7:25; 1 John 5:12)

_____

15. Reviewing how you receive His life, put Romans 10:13 in your own words.

_____

_____

_____

16. When you give yourself fully to the Lord Jesus Christ, how are you seen by God? Colossians 3:3 (Philippians 3:9)

_____

17. What human experience illustrates the manner in which you are identified with the name of Christ? Romans 7:4 (Matthew 22:2)

_____

18. In token of your new association, how are you called? Acts 11:26 (1 Peter 4:16)

_____

19. How should you live now in keeping with your new name? Colossians 3:17 (Ephesians 5:20)

_____

Make Your Own Application

Prayer is your greatest privilege. It is through the prayer of faith that you are saved when you call upon the name of the Lord. And it is prayer in His name that sustains your life thereafter. In this connection, read John 14:13, 14 and 16:23, 24. After you have thought about the meaning of prayer, write out what you understand the name of Christ to mean, and why God promises you anything in His name.

_____

_____

_____

_____

_____

_____

_____

_____

_____

_____

_____

_____

Memorize Romans 10:9; Hebrews 7:25

The other evening as I was riding home after a heavy day's work, I felt weary and sore depressed when swiftly, suddenly, as a lightning flash, came: "My grace is sufficient for thee."

And I said: "I should think it is, Lord," and burst out laughing. I never fully understood what the holy laughter of Abraham was until then. It seemed to make unbelief so absurd.

It was as if some little fish, being very thirsty, was troubled about drinking the river dry; and Father Thames said: "Drink away, little fish, my stream is sufficient for thee." Or it seemed like a little mouse in the granaries of Egypt after seven years of plenty, fearing it might die of famine, and Joseph might say: "Cheer up, little mouse, my granaries are sufficient for thee."

Again, I imagined a man away up on yonder mountain saying to himself: "I fear I shall exhaust all the oxygen in the atmosphere. But the earth might say: "Breathe away, O man, and fill thy lungs; my atmosphere is sufficient for thee."

O brethren, be great believers! Little faith will bring your soul to Heaven, but great faith will bring Heaven to you.

—C. H. SPURGEON

There is a fountain filled with blood
    Drawn from Immanuel's veins,
And sinners plunged beneath that flood
    Lose all their guilty stains:
Dear dying Lamb, Thy precious blood
    Shall never lose its pow'r,
Till all the ransomed Church of God
    Be saved to sin no more:
E'er since by faith I saw the stream
    Thy flowing wounds supply,
Redeeming love has been my theme
    And shall be till I die.

—WILLIAM COWPER

Faith is not hope, not a mere expectation of future things, but a present receiving of that which is promised——in a real and substantial way. It is accepting, not expecting! It is not sight, for it deals with things not seen. The region of the visible is not the realm of faith. When a thing is proved by demonstration, it is a matter not of faith but of evidence. Faith asks no other evidence than God's Word, and its own assurance. It is the evidence.

——A. B. SIMPSON

In wonder lost, with trembling joy,
  We take the pardon of our God:
Pardon for crimes of deepest dye,
  A pardon bought with Jesu's blood,
Who is a pardoning God like Thee?
Or who has grace so rich and free?

O may this strange, this matchless grace,
  This God-like miracle of love,
Fill the whole earth with grateful praise,
  And all th'angelic choirs above!
Who is a pardoning God like Thee?
Or who has grace so rich and free?

——SAMUEL DAVIES

A wise bird knows that a scarecrow is simply an advertisement. It announces in the most forceful and picturesque way that in the garden which it does its best to adorn, some very juicy and delicious fruit is to be had for the picking. Every thoughtful bird learns in time to regard a scarecrow as an invitation to a banquet. He feels as a hungry man feels when he hears the dinner bell ring. . . . Faith is a bird which loves to perch on scarecrows. She knows that there are scarecrows wherever there are strawberries.

——FRANK BOREHAM

JUSTIFIED FREELY

Do you believe that you appear before God free from all sin? Such a thing sounds incredible in view of your human failings. But when you think of your position in Christ, it is altogether reasonable. In fact, where there is any sense of condemnation for sin in your heart it can be due only to ignorance of the benefits of His redemption or disobedience to His will.

Christ "put away sin by the sacrifice of himself" (Hebrews 9:26). That settled it so far as God's justice is concerned, and when by faith you lay hold upon its completeness, then all your sins are canceled, and before God your record is clear. You are "justified from all things" (Acts 13:39), which means that you stand in the same relation to God as if you had never sinned. In turn, the righteousness of Christ is imputed to you, so that you are "made the righteousness of God in him" (2 Corinthians 5:21).

All this happens the moment you turn from sin and receive by faith the gift of God's grace. Justification is no sentence extending through years of struggle, nor is it something you realize after death. There is, of course, a progressive growth in the knowledge and grace of God, and your obedient walk of faith is continuous, but the actual work of God's pardoning grace becomes effective instantaneously with faith.

Where this is understood, what a relief it gives to your soul! You may have to bear the reproach for past sins and present mistakes, but the guilt is gone, and in its place is peace—abiding peace with God and man. "If the Son therefore shall make you free, ye shall be free indeed" (John 8:36).

Remember, however, that the moral law of God is still binding on your conduct, and your freedom is never license to sin. You are free from sin but in bondage to Christ, and in His righteousness you are to "go, and sin no more" (John 8:11).

In whom we have redemption through his blood, even the forgiveness of sins.

Colossians 1:14

Therefore, being justified by faith, we have peace with God through our Lord Jesus Christ.

Romans 5:1

Find It For Yourself

1. What happened to your sins when Christ died on the cross? Hebrews 9:26 (1 John 3:5)

_____

2. Where were your sins put when He took them away? Colossians 2:14

_____

3. Because Christ was made sin for you, what are you made in Him? 2 Corinthians 5:21

_____

4. In what then does your righteousness consist? Romans 3:22; 10:3, 4

_____

5. How is His righteousness received and kept? Romans 1:17; 3:25 (Hebrews 10:38, 39)

_____

6. Why is faith and faith alone the means by which you are made righteous? Romans 4:2–5 (Ephesians 2:9)

_____

_____

_____

7. How are you thus legally regarded by God? Romans 3:24 (Acts 13:39)

---

8. As one justified by faith, what is your relationship now to the law which once condemned you? Romans 7:6 (Galatians 5:1)

---

9. How does this affect your old sense of guilt incurred by the law? Romans 8:1, 2 (John 5:24)

---

10. As to your past sins, what are you assured of by virtue of Christ's redeeming work? Ephesians 1:7 (Colossians 1:14)

---

11. How many of your sins does God forgive? Colossians 2:13 (1 John 1:9)

---

12. What does it mean to forgive sins as far as God is concerned? Hebrews 10:17 (Isaiah 43:25)

---

13. How should this knowledge of forgiveness affect your own inner feeling? Romans 5:1 (1 John 3:21)

---

14. What must you do in order to keep your peace and assurance as you live by faith? John 5:14; 8:11 (Romans 6:12)

---

15. What are you obligated to obey in your freedom from sin? Romans 6:18, 19 (Ephesians 6:6)

_____

16. Write out in your own words 1 Peter 2:16.

_____

_____

_____

_____

_____

17. If you are content to go on living in known sin, what does it indicate about your life? 1 John 3:9 (John 8:34; Hebrews 10:29)

_____

18. In your effort to do what is right, how are you expected to treat those whom you have wronged? Ezekiel 33:14, 15 (Luke 19:8)

_____

19. On the other hand, what must you do to those who have wronged you? Ephesians 4:32 (Colossians 3:13; Mark 11:25)

_____

20. To sum it up from a practical standpoint, who are those who are really sincere regarding their righteousness in Christ? 1 John 3:7 (James 1:25-27)

_____

_____

_____

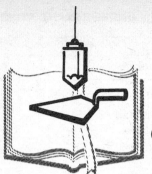

Make Your Own Application

Read Romans 1:16, 17, and after reflecting upon what it means to say "the just shall live by faith," briefly tell why living this way makes you righteous.

_____

_____

_____

_____

_____

_____

_____

_____

_____

_____

_____

_____

Memorize Colossians 1:14; Romans 5:1

Sons of God, triumphant rise,
Shout th' accomplished sacrifice!
Shout your sins in Christ forgiven,
Sons of God, and heirs of heaven!

Ye that round our altars throng,
List'ning angels, join the song:
Sing with us, ye heavenly powers,
Pardon, grace, and glory, ours.

Love's mysterious work is done:
Greet we now th' atoning Son:
Healed and quickened by his blood,
Joined to Christ, and one with God.

Him by faith we taste below,
Mightier joys ordained to know,
When his utmost grace we prove,
Rise to heaven by perfect love.

——CHARLES WESLEY

Any man can sing by day; but only he whose heart has been tuned by the gracious hand of Jehovah can sing in the darkness. The things of earth may satisfy for the hours of prosperity; but only the peace of God can give gladness in the darkness of adversity. God gives joy in sorrow; and when the sad one sings through his tears, then the Lord comes out to him with new and more tender assurances, so that by his very hymn he is made more gladsome. That which is born of trust rises in rapture.

——WM. M. TAYLOR

An old Scottish woman who was alone for the greater part of each day was asked what she did during the day. "Well," she replied, "I get my hymn book, and I have a little hymn of praise to the Lord." "Then," she added, "I get my Bible and let the Lord speak to me. When I am tired of reading, and I cannot sing anymore, I just sit still and let the Lord love me."

Have you ever noted the Master's mathematics in these two sparrow texts—Matthew 10:29 and Luke 12:6? The sparrow was sold as an article of food in the Palestine markets. So cheap was the little bird that two of them were sold for the paltry pittance of a farthing. "Are not two sparrows sold for a farthing?" "Are not five sparrows sold for two farthings?" Naturally four of them would be sold for two farthings. But so insignificant were they in the sight of the vendor that, when a buyer came along with two farthings, the seller threw in an extra one, giving five for two, instead of four. Yet of this extra sparrow—almost worthless in the sight of the vendor—the Lord utters this wonderful word, "Not one of them is forgotten before God."

We have been missing a wondrous truth. The God of the universe is also the God of the tiny sparrow. As that sparrow is ever before the face of God, and in His tender care, so the most trivial details of our lives are ever present, unforgotten, and tenderly cared for before our Father in heaven. He wants us to bring every such detail, however insignificant, in the happy confidence that He is ever watching and waiting to meet our every need however humble."

—J. H. MCCONKEY

Children of the heavenly King,
As we journey let us sing;
Sing our Savior's worthy praise,
Glorious in His works and ways.

Fear not, brethren; joyful stand
On the borders of our land;
Jesus Christ, our Father's Son,
Bids us undismayed go on.

Lord, obediently we'll go,
Gladly leaving all below;
Only Thou our Leader be,
And we still will follow Thee.

—JOHN CENNICK

A CHILD OF THE KING

Do you feel the thrill of belonging to the King's family? You certainly should, for when you receive Christ, you are adopted into the very household of God. All the rights and privileges of a royal son are yours. In loving confidence you can look up into the face of your great Creator and say, "Abba, Father" (Romans 8:15).

God has always wanted it this way. He created you in His image that He might have pleasure in your fellowship. But because of sin, your original likeness was ruined and your relationship to Him was lost. You were "alienated . . . in your mind by wicked works" (Colossians 1:21) and became a stranger to the covenant of promise. Nevertheless, God loved you for what He meant you to be in Christ, and moved by that love, He sent His Son into the world to make reconciliation. Christ died to abolish "in his flesh the enmity" (Ephesians 2:15) caused by your sin, and thereby made it possible for you to come back within the circle of His family.

Recognize, however, that you still live in an alien world. It does not know the Fatherhood of God and so cannot offer you the brotherhood of man. Bound by Satan it will never be your friend, nor can you be its companion. As a Christian, of course, you must be willing to accept your place of responsibility in society, and ever seek to lift the burdens of those ensnared by sin, but this world is not your home.

You belong to another family. All the redeemed of the ages are your kinsmen. Christ is your elder Brother, and God Almighty is your Father in heaven. So hold your head high and walk as becomes a child of the King.

And because ye are sons, God hath sent forth the Spirit of his Son into your hearts, crying, Abba, Father.

Galatians 4:6

And all things are of God, who hath reconciled us to himself by Jesus Christ, and hath given to us the ministry of reconciliation.

2 Corinthians 5:18

Find It For Yourself

1. What family relationship do you have in Christ? Galatians 3:26 (1 John 3:1)

_____

2. When are you considered a child of God? John 1:12 (1 John 3:2)

_____

3. What were you before becoming a child of God? Ephesians 2:12 (Colossians 1:21; Matthew 15:8)

_____

4. How were you reconciled to God? Ephesians 2:13, 16 (Hebrews 2:17; 2 Corinthians 5:18)

_____

5. Explain what it means to be "reconciled" to God. Ephesians 2:14, 15 (Colossians 1:20)

_____

_____

6. What privilege does reconciliation give you? Ephesians 2:18 (Romans 5:2)

_____

_____

7. What was the legal way by which you became a member of the family of God? Galatians 4:5 (Romans 8:15)

_____

8. As an adopted child, how do you now address God? Galatians 4:6 (Romans 8:17)

_____

9. The Bible is full of pictures of how precious you are to your Father. How are you described in:
   Malachi 3:17

   _____

   Zechariah 2:8

   _____

   Isaiah 62:3

   _____

10. Yet your loving Father may give you spankings. Why? Hebrews 12:5–11

   _____

11. When you are reproved by the Spirit of God, what must you do? Revelation 3:19 (1 John 1:9)

   _____

12. As long as you obey your Father, what will continue to be your experience with Christ? 1 John 1:7 (John 8:12)

   _____

   _____

13. How do you stand out in the world when you keep in step with God? Philippians 2:15 (1 Thessalonians 5:5)

_____

_____

14. How is your fellowship with God expressed in your attitude toward your fellowmen? 1 John 2:10, 11 (Matthew 22:37–39)

_____

_____

15. How may you be regarded by the world because of your relationship with Christ? John 17:14 (1 John 3:13)

_____

_____

16. Though you are not at home in this world, what does Christ give to bless your soul? John 17:13 (Romans 14:4)

_____

17. What danger must you guard against in the world? John 17:15 (Ephesians 5:11)

_____

18. As a child of God, what is your greatest desire for every person in the world? 1 John 1:3 (Acts 17:27)

_____

_____

_____

Make Your Own Application

Read carefully 1 John 3:10–24. Note how the children of God are different from the children of the devil. As you look at your own life, mention several ways in which you see the difference.

_____

_____

_____

_____

_____

_____

_____

_____

_____

_____

_____

_____

Memorize Galatians 4:6; 2 Corinthians 5:18

Christian, fear not to claim God's promises to make you holy. Listen not to the suggestion that the corruption of your old nature would render holiness an impossibility. In your flesh dwells no good thing, and that flesh, though crucified with Christ, is not yet dead, but will continually seek to rise and lead you to evil. But the Father is the Husbandman. He has grafted the life of Christ on your life. That holy life is mightier than your evil life; under the watchful care of the Husbandman, that new life can keep down the workings of the evil life within you.

And now, if you would live a holy life, abide in Christ your sanctification. Look upon Him as the Holy One of God, made man that He might communicate to us the holiness of God. Listen when Scripture teaches that there is within you a new nature, a new man, created in Christ Jesus in righteousness and true holiness. Remember that this holy nature which is in you is singularly fitted for living a holy life, and performing all holy duties, as much so as the old nature is for doing evil. Understand that this holy nature within you has its root and life in Christ in heaven, and can only grow and become strong as the intercourse between it and its source is uninterrupted. And above all, believe most confidently that Jesus Christ Himself delights in maintaining that new nature within you, and imparting to it His own strength and wisdom for its work. Let that faith lead you daily to the surrender of all self-confidence, and the confession of the utter corruption of all there is in you by nature. Let it fill you with a quiet and assured confidence that you are indeed able to do what the Father expects of you as His child, under the covenant of His grace, because you have Christ strengthening you. Let it teach you to lay yourself and your services on the altar as spiritual sacrifices, holy and acceptable in His sight, a sweet-smelling savour. Look not upon a life of holiness as a strain and an effort, but as the natural outgrowth of the life of Christ within you. And let ever again a quiet, hopeful, gladsome faith hold itself assured that all you need for a holy life will most assuredly be given you out of the holiness of Jesus.

—ANDREW MURRAY

Take time to be holy, speak oft with thy Lord;
Abide in Him always and feed on His Word.
Make friends of God's children, help those who are weak,
Forgetting in nothing His blessing to seek.

Take time to be holy, the world rushes on;
Spend much time in secret with Jesus alone.
By looking to Jesus, like Him thou shalt be;
Thy friends in thy conduct His likeness shall see.

Take time to be holy, let Him be thy guide,
And run not before Him, whatever betide.
In joy or in sorrow still follow thy Lord,
And, looking to Jesus, still trust in his Word.

Take time to be holy, be calm in thy soul—
Each thought and each motive beneath His control.
Thus led by His Spirit to fountains of love,
Thou soon shalt be fitted for service above.

—WILLIAM D. LONGSTAFF

It is a great deal better to live a holy life than to talk about it. Lighthouses do not ring bells and fire cannons to call attention to their shining. They just shine!

—DWIGHT L. MOODY

MADE HOLY

Do you realize that in receiving the Holy Spirit you partake of the holiness of Christ? That's right. It could be no other way. The vessel that God indwells must be holy, for that is His nature. Every area of your life that the Spirit possesses is sanctified or set apart for God's use. You are created after His design "in righteousness and true holiness" (Ephesians 4:24).

Understand, however, that the holiness which you have is by virtue of His control of your life, and is always conditioned upon your knowledge of His will and your willingness to let Him have His way. The more you understand how His perfect life relates to you, the more you will be able to experience His holiness. Of course, you can never be perfect in knowledge because of your human limitations. But to the degree that you do understand His will, you can be perfect in love while at the same time you desire to know more of His perfection.

Doubtless many corrections will be called for in your life as you grow in understanding of His nature. Unclean habits, stubborn prejudices, neglected duties, even your selfish "carnal" disposition of enmity and pride depriving you of the Spirit's fullness will come under His condemnation. But whatever it is, when it is seen to be sin, confess it to God, and appropriate by faith the cleansing power of the blood.

The Spirit is faithfully striving to bring your character in line with his. He wants you to be like Jesus. Never grieve Him by letting something linger in your heart which is known to be contrary to His nature. And as you obediently walk in His light, fully committed to Christ, you will continue to be conformed to His likeness. In this devotion, though not faultless, you can be preserved "blameless" unto the coming again of your Lord (1 Thessalonians 5:23).

Now we have received, not the spirit of the world, but the spirit which is of God; that we might know the things that are freely given to us of God.
1 Corinthians 2:12

Sanctify them through thy truth: thy word is truth.
John 17:17

Find It For Yourself

1. What is there about the new life in Christ which makes you live holy in deed as well as in name? Ephesians 4:24 (Colossians 3:10)

---

2. What is the spiritual work called whereby you are made holy and set apart for God? Ephesians 5:26 (2 Thessalonians 2:13)

---

3. What is the basis for your sanctification? Hebrews 10:14; 13:12 (Ephesians 5:26)

---

4. Like everything else about your salvation, how does the sanctification which Christ earned become yours? Hebrews 10:22 (Acts 15:9)

---

5. What does the Spirit give to make your life different? Romans 5:5 (1 John 4:16)

---

6. What other fruits of righteousness does the Spirit bring forth in your life? Galatians 5:22, 23 (Ephesians 5:9)

---

7. In contrast, what marks of your old life must you be careful to avoid? Ephesians 4:25–29 (Colossians 3:8, 9)

_____

_____

_____

8. What can still remain in your nature as a Christian to cause you trouble? 1 Corinthians 3:3 (Hebrews 12:15)

_____

9. How is this fleshly nature recognized? Romans 7:22, 24; 8:7

_____

_____

10. What must you do with any sinful practices or attitudes of the flesh? 2 Corinthians 7:1 (2 Timothy 2:21)

_____

11. Believing that the work of Christ is adequate and available for every need, how are you cleansed from sin when you see it in your life? 1 John 1:9

_____

12. In practical terms, what must happen to make any area of your life holy for God's use? Exodus 30:29; Matthew 23:19 (Romans 12:1)

_____

13. To put it another way, what enables you to have a pure soul, regardless of what your measure of light may be? 1 Peter 1:22 (Acts 5:32)

_____

_____

14. Sum up the secret of God's continual cleansing and fellowship according to 1 John 1:7.

_____

_____

15. Thus how may you serve the Lord all the days of your life? Luke 1:75 (Hebrews 12:14)

_____

16. What is the measure of a life full and running over with Christ? Ephesians 5:18 (Acts 2:4)

_____

17. As long as you obey whatever truth the Spirit shows you, how is your character preserved in this life? 1 Thessalonians 5:23

_____

_____

18. When at last Christ returns at the end of the world, how will you be presented unto His glory? Jude 24 (Revelation 14:5)

_____

_____

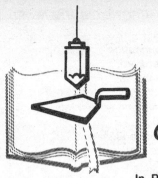

Make Your Own Application

In Philippians 3:12 the Apostle Paul says that he is not perfect, and in Philippians 3:15 he says he is perfect. Explain from the context the two ways this word is to be interpreted in experience, and cite an example of it in your own life.

_____
_____
_____
_____
_____
_____
_____
_____
_____
_____
_____
_____
_____
_____

Memorize 1 Corinthians 2:12; John 17:17

The church's one foundation
   Is Jesus Christ her Lord;
She is His new creation
   By water and the Word:
From heaven He came and sought her
   To be His holy Bride;
With His own blood He bought her,
   And for her life He died.

Elect from every nation,
   Yet one o'er all the earth,
Her charter of salvation,
   One Lord, one Faith, one Birth,
One Holy Name she blesses,
   Partakes one Holy Food,
And to one hope she presses,
   With every grace endued.

Though with a scornful wonder
   Men see her sore opprest,
By schisms rent asunder,
   By heresies distrest,
Yet saints their watch are keeping,
   Their cry goes up, "How long?"
And soon the night of weeping
   Shall be the morn of song.

'Mid toil and tribulation,
   And tumult of her war,
She waits the consummation
   Of peace forevermore;
Till with the vision glorious
   Her longing eyes are blest,
And the great Church victorious
   Shall be the Church at rest.

Yet she on earth hath union
 With God the Three in One,
And mystic sweet communion
 With those whose rest is won;
O happy ones and holy!
 Lord, give us grace, that we,
Like them, the meek and lowly,
 On high may dwell with Thee.

——SAMUEL J. STONE

We love ourselves, because we are members of Jesus Christ. We love Jesus Christ, because He is the body of which we are members. All is one, one is in the other, like the Three Persons.

——BLAISE PASCAL

The scandal of our divisions is not, as we are told to believe, the mere existence of separate denominations as such. That we come from different schools, refer to different headquarters, adhere to different forms of worship, ministry and government, is not in itself hurting the Body of Christ or grieving the Holy Spirit. The real scandal, right across all denominations and within each one of them, is the absence of the gospel from our pulpits, the uncertain sound of the trumpet at the moment of battle, the chaos of conflicting voices that makes it impossible for men to hear what the Spirit says unto the churches. Accordingly, prayer for unity is not petition for merger schemes, but "that all who profess and call themselves Christians may agree in the truth of Thy holy Word and live in unity and godly love."

——FRANZ HILDEBRANDT

Lesson 12

UNITED WITH THE CHURCH

Isn't it wonderful to know that you belong to "the holy catholic church"? This fact should thrill you, for it means that you are a member of the universal assembly of those "called out" of the world and translated into the kingdom of Christ. You do not join it by reciting a creed, nor do you build it by good deeds; you enter it by divine grace through the new birth. All who have ever lived by faith in the Son of God—past, present, and future—are included in this great "communion of saints."

Christ Himself is the Head of the church, "which is his body, the fulness of him that filleth all in all" (Ephesians 1:23). As such, the church is not an organization of men, but an organism of the Spirit. "There is one body, and one Spirit . . . one Lord, one faith, one baptism, one God and Father of all" (Ephesians 4:4–6). Each member is different "according to the measure of the gift of Christ" (Ephesians 4:7), yet each one has some vital function in the life of the whole body, and all together grow up in the stature of Him whose life they share.

Thank God, the church is undivided. This unity, of course, is spiritual, and is not seen in any physical structure or organization. Denominational differences within the visible church today do not repudiate our essential oneness in the Spirit. Furthermore, efforts to get everyone together in one super church organization may be as dangerous as they are artificial.

However, to the degree that the particular congregation of believers of which you are a part manifests the true Spirit of God, that church is a visible expression of the body of Christ in this world. Though beset with all the limitations of the flesh, it is still the best institution that God has on this earth. Guard its reputation as you would your Lord's. It is His bride, and someday he intends to present it unto Himself "a glorious church" (Ephesians 5:27), when all its members are "made perfect in one" (John 17:23).

And let us consider one another to provoke unto love and to good works: not forsaking the assembling of ourselves together, as the manner of some is; but exhorting one another: and so much the more, as ye see the day approaching.

Hebrews 10:24, 25

I in them, and thou in me, that they may be made perfect in one; and that the world may know that thou hast sent me, and hast loved them, as thou has loved me.

John 17:23

Find It For Yourself

1. When does one become a member of the church in the New Testament? Acts 2:47 (Acts 5:14; 11:21; 14:1)

_____

2. What do you come into when you enter the true church? Hebrews 12:22, 23

_____

3. If the church is composed of all saved people, how is it recognized in the Old Testament days? Galatians 6:16 (Deuteronomy 32:9; Ezekiel 34:15)

_____

4. How is this eternal fellowship described in relation to the government of God? Hebrews 12:28 (John 18:36)

_____

5. In its spiritual and invisible essence, how is the church described? Colossians 1:18 (Ephesians 1:23)

_____

6. How are you related through the Spirit to all other members of the body of Christ? 1 Corinthians 12:12–20 (Ephesians 4:4)

_____

_____

7. What then constitutes the unity of the church? 1 Corinthians 12:13 (Ephesians 4:3–6)

_____

_____

8. What character does this spiritual kingdom have that distinguishes its members? Romans 14:17 (Acts 15:9)

_____

9. How is the church continued in the apostolic succession? Acts 2:42 (1 Corinthians 3:10, 11)

_____

_____

10. What must you do among yourselves as you follow the teachings and mission of the apostles? Philippians 2:2 (Ephesians 4:3)

_____

_____

11. How should you feel when something happens to another member of the church? 1 Corinthians 12:25, 26 (Galatians 6:2)

_____

_____

12. In practical terms, what must you do in the local church to fulfill your responsibility? Hebrews 10:24, 25 (Acts 2:46)

_____

_____

13. How does God provide for the different needs of His people within the church organization? 1 Corinthians 12:4–11 (Romans 12:6–8)

_____

_____

14. What should you do with any gift that God gives? Romans 12:6–8 (2 Timothy 1:6)

_____

_____

15. What must you be careful to avoid in the church? 2 Corinthians 12:20 (1 Corinthians 1:11)

_____

_____

16. Where strife and unconcern do come into the church, what must you do to experience newness of life? 2 Chronicles 7:14 (Psalms 85:6)

_____

_____

17. To what can you compare the love that Christ has for His church? Ephesians 5:25 (Revelation 19:7)

_____

_____

18. How does Christ intend someday to present His bride, the church? Ephesians 5:27 (John 17:23)

_____

_____

_____

Make Your Own Application

Jesus said that His church was established upon an indestructible foundation. Review the circumstances which called forth this promise as recorded in Matthew 16:16–18 and tell why nothing shall ever prevail against it.

_____
_____
_____
_____
_____
_____
_____
_____
_____
_____
_____
_____
_____
_____

Memorize Hebrews 10:24, 25; John 17:23

When we are asked how many ministers our church has, the traditional answer is "one" or "five," depending on how large the paid staff is. But the real answer is "200" or "2,000," depending on how large the membership is, for every believer is a minister. When we are asked, "Where is your church?" the traditional reply is, "On the corner of Broad and Main." But the correct reply is, "What time is it?" If it is 11:00 a.m. Sunday, then our church is "on the corner of Broad and Main." (That is where the headquarters building is.) But if it is 11:00 a.m. Tuesday, then our church is Room 511 in the Professional Building, where Bill White, Christian attorney, is practicing law. It is at 3009 Melody Lane, where Jane White, Christian housewife, is making a home. It is at Central High, where Jimmy White, Christian student, is studying to the glory of God. There is the church in action!

——RICHARD HALVERSON

I expect to pass through this life but once. If there is any kindness or any good thing I can do to my fellow-beings, let me do it now. I shall pass this way but once.

——AN OLD QUAKER

Attempt great things for God: expect great things from God.

——WILLIAM CAREY

Give me one hundred preachers who fear nothing but sin and desire nothing but God, and I care not a straw whether they be clergymen or laymen, such alone will shake the gates of hell and set up the kingdom of heaven upon earth.

——JOHN WESLEY

We do not argue about worldliness; we witness. We do not discuss philosophy; we preach the Gospel. We do not speculate about the destiny of sinners; we pluck them as brands from the burning.

——SAMUEL CHADWICK

Lord, give to me Thy love for souls
For lost and wand'ring sheep,
That I may see the multitude
And weep as Thou didst weep.

Help me to see the tragic plight
Of souls far off in sin;
Help me to love, to pray, and go
To bring the wand'ring in.

From off the altar of Thy heart
Take Thou some flaming coals,
Then touch my life and give me, Lord,
A heart that's hot for souls.

O fire of love, O flame Divine
Make Thy abode in me;
Burn in my heart, burn evermore,
Till I burn out for Thee.

——EUGENE M. HARRISON

Oh, Lord, give me a back bone as big as a saw log, and ribs like the sleepers under the church floor; put iron shoes on me, and galvanized breeches. Give me a rhinocerous hide for a skin, and hang a wagon load of determination up in the gable-end of my soul, and help me to sign the contract to fight the devil as long as I've got a fist, and bite him as long as I've got a tooth, and then gum him till I die. All this I ask for Christ's sake. Amen.

——BUD ROBINSON

Lesson 13

MINISTER OF GOD

Do you realize that you are a minister of Christ? Yes, regardless of your particular vocation, you minister before God and man with the authority of a priest and the dignity of a king (Revelation 1:6). What is more, you don't have to go through any mortal person or ceremony to reach the throne of heaven. Christ is now your reigning High Priest, and along with every other true believer, you partake of His "holy priesthood, to offer up spiritual sacrifices, acceptable to God by Jesus Christ" (1 Peter 2:5).

When this truth is revealed to you, you realize that Christian service is not something reserved only for a few pious saints or ordained clergymen in the church. It is the duty of every child of God. Some people are specially chosen for full-time work in the church, but all Christians are called to serve in the general "work of the ministry" (Ephesians 4:12).

In this sense, you are today the actual representative of God ministering "in Christ's stead" (2 Corinthians 5:20). As the Father sent the Son, now Christ sends you to continue in your body the service which He did in His body (John 20:21). Viewed this way, you are His hands and feet seeking those He died to save. The relationship which you have with His work is so complete that what is done to you in your service is regarded as though it were done to Christ Himself (Matthew 10:40).

Remember, though, that the servant is never above his Lord (Matthew 10:24). Ministering selflessly for others is a sacrifical work. It cost Jesus His life. And it will cost yours——at least, it will mean the denial of your own rights in loving surrender to His cross. Yet in giving your life, you will find it (Matthew 10:39), and in serving others for whom He gave His life, you will experience the joy of His own ministry.

Then said Jesus to them again, Peace be unto you: as my Father hath sent me, even so send I you.
John 20:21

For whosoever will save his life shall lose it; but whosoever shall lose his life for my sake and the gospel's, the same shall save it.
Mark 8:35

Find It For Yourself

1. What are you made in relation to God through Christ? 1 Peter 2:5 (Revelation 1:6; Isaiah 61:6)

_____

_____

2. Why can you come before God any time and offer spiritual sacrifices? Hebrews 4:14–16 (Romans 8:34)

_____

_____

3. What should continually characterize your prayers? Hebrews 13:15 (1 Peter 2:9)

_____

4. In relation to your fellowmen, how do you minister to God? Matthew 25:35–40 (John 21:16)

_____

_____

5. While every Christian is a priest unto God and a minister to his fellowmen, what are some specially called to be in the church? Ephesians 4:11 (1 Corinthians 12:28)

_____

_____

6. What does the pastor and teacher train the saints to do? Ephesians 4:12

_____

7. To what official position are Christians appointed in this world? 2 Corinthians 5:20 (1 Timothy 1:12)

_____

8. What keeps urging you on in this service? 2 Corinthians 5:14 (John 13:35)

_____

9. Who is always there personally to comfort and sustain you in your ministry for Christ? John 14:16 (Acts 9:31)

_____

10. What is the importance which Christ puts upon your service in His name? Matthew 10:40 (Luke 10:16)

_____

11. How should the honor and responsibility which Christ has placed upon you affect your attitude toward yourself? James 4:10 (2 Peter 5:5; Matthew 18:4)

_____

12. What is the standard for service to remember in all that you do? Acts 20:35 (Matthew 10:8)

_____

13. Some people have more ability than others; so how is your service measured by Christ? Luke 12:48 (Mark 14:8)

_____

_____

14. How should you face the hardships that come to you? 2 Timothy 2:3, 4 (Hebrews 13:13)

_____

15. How do you put to silence the ignorance of foolish men who reproach you? 1 Peter 2:15 (Romans 12:20)

_____

16. Describing what your soul experiences when you take the yoke of Christ, write a free translation of Matthew 11:29.

_____

_____

_____

_____

_____

17. How will the needs that arise in your life be supplied? Philippians 4:19 (Luke 6:38; Matthew 6:33)

_____

18. What wages do you receive for your work in the kingdom? John 4:36 (1 Thessalonians 2:19, 20)

_____

19. In the end, what will be the reward for your faithfulness? Matthew 25:23 (Luke 12:43, 44)

_____

20. What should you always be busy doing, since you know that your labor is not in vain in the Lord? 1 Corinthians 15:58 (Hebrews 13:16)

_____

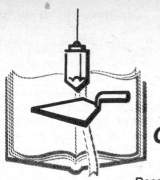

Make Your Own Application

Recalling the Great Commission of your Lord in Matthew 28:19, 20 and Mark 16:15, meditate upon John 14:12. Then state several ways in which you are endeavoring to do the work of Christ.

_____

_____

_____

_____

_____

_____

_____

_____

_____

_____

_____

Memorize John 20:21; Mark 8:35

Perchance you have never seen God's byway for your life. But here is a greater truth. For running all the way through this Book of God, and blazoned upon every page of it is a great highway. It is the highway of consecration. It is for all believers. No man who walks in this highway need ever fear missing God's byway. And the reason most men are missing the particular call of God to their own personal life-work is because they have never obeyed the general call of God to all believers to enter upon this highway of dedication to Him. "If any man will to do My will he shall know the teaching," is an absolute promise of guidance to the child of God who yields his own will to do the will of God.

—JAMES H. MCCONKEY

He leadeth me; O blessed thought!
O words with heavenly comfort fraught!
Whate'er I do, where'er I be,
Still 'tis God's hand that leadeth me.

Sometimes mid scenes of deepest gloom,
Sometimes where Eden's bowers bloom,
By waters still, o'er troubled sea,
Still 'tis God's hand that leadeth me.

Lord, I would place my hand in thine,
Nor ever murmur nor repine;
Content, whatever lot I see,
Since 'tis my God that leadeth me.

—JOSEPH H. GILMORE

People who study and understand birds know they fly much higher when migrating than when in local flight. They concluded that migrating birds take wing higher than the others for three reasons: they get a boundless view and more easily find their points of direction; they are out of the flight path of birds of prey and clear of obstacles; and their flight is accelerated due to the greater depuration of the atmosphere. The higher the child of God soars the more clearly discernible is God's flight plan.

——MRS. CHARLES E. COWMAN

Few are needed to do the out-of-the-way tasks which startle the world, and one may be most useful just doing commonplace duties, and leaving the issue with God. And when it is all over, and our feet will run no more, and our hands are helpless, and we have scarcely strength to murmur a last prayer, then we shall see that, instead of needing a larger field, we have left untilled many corners of our single acre, and that none of it is fit for our Master's eye were it not for the softening shadow of the Cross.

——GEORGE MACDONALD

He writes in characters too grand
For our short sight to understand;
We catch but broken strokes, and try
To fathom all the mystery
Of withered hopes, of death, of life,
The endless war, the useless strife——
But there, with larger, dearer sight
We shall see this——His way was right.

——JOHN OXENHAM

All through the Bible there is a wonderful care of little things, God noticing them and bringing them to perfectness of meaning. "He putteth my tears in his bottle"; that is condescension. "None of his steps shall slide," as if He numbered step by step all the going of His people. One of those people said, "Thou knowest my downsitting and mine uprising," and "Thou hast beset me behind and before."

——JOSEPH PARKER

Lesson 14

DIVINE GUIDANCE

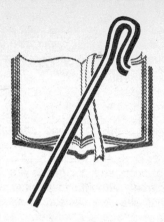

Do you sense that God is leading you like a Shepherd? This is your promise. He has given you His Spirit to "guide you into all truth" (John 16:13). Clearly your Savior does not want you to be without His personal direction in the decisions that must be made in the course of life.

But you must be willing to follow. This means the complete surrender of your will to His. Most of the confusion in the Christian life comes because this point is not clear. You simply cannot know God's leading when you are determined to have your own way. Only as you offer yourself "a living sacrifice," and maintain that dedication through "the renewing of your mind," can you "prove what is that good, and acceptable, and perfect, will of God" (Romans 12:1, 2).

Once this problem is settled, you must seek to know what God's will is for your life in any given situation, and you will be required to expend some real effort on your part. God does not give to you what you are able to get for yourself. Lazy Christians are always in the dark. You need to avail yourself of every means at hand to get instruction. Study the Bible. Pray for guidance. Counsel with other Christians. Use common sense.

Through these disciplines, the Spirit will show you something to do. He may not guide you to answers for your entire future, but you will know enough to take at least the next step. And acting upon all that you do understand now to be His will, howsoever small the insight may be, you will increasingly discover new meaning and purpose as you go along.

Your way will not always be easy. You may pass through some dark valleys and experience many trials to your faith. But through it all, the Lord will go with you. You need have no fear. He knows the way.

For as many as are led by the Spirit of God, they are the sons of God.

Romans 8:14

And we know that all things work together for good to them that love God, to them who are the called according to his purpose.

Romans 8:28

Find It For Yourself

1. What is your confidence as you face new decisions every day? Isaiah 48:17 (Psalms 48:14)

   _____

2. What can you compare God to in respect to His leadership? Psalms 23:1 (John 10:3, 4)

   _____

3. What does your Shepherd do for you when the way gets dark? Luke 1:79 (Isaiah 42:16)

   _____

4. Which person of the Trinity acts as your Guide now? Romans 8:14 (John 14:26)

   _____

5. What does the Spirit of God lead you to know? John 16:13 (1 John 5:6)

   _____

6. That the Spirit will show you truth is certain, but what is your responsibility in finding it? Luke 11:9, 10 (Jeremiah 29:13)

   _____

7. How does the Spirit help you pray when you are sincerely seeking truth? Romans 8:26, 27 (John 16:15)

_____

_____

8. What would be a good way to pray whenever you are facing some decision? Psalms 25:5; 31:3; 143:10 (Ezra 7:10)

_____

_____

9. In regard to your own life, what must you first of all be willing for God to show you? Psalms 139:23, 24 (Proverbs 28:13)

_____

_____

10. Where is the best place to go to find truth? Psalms 119:105, 130 (2 Timothy 3:16)

_____

11. How must you use the Scriptures for them to speak to you? Acts 17:11 (2 Timothy 2:15)

_____

12. What else can you do to safeguard your decisions? Proverbs 11:14 (Matthew 18:19, 20)

_____

13. Where do children especially receive their direction and nurture? Ephesians 6:4 (Deuteronomy 6:7)

_____

14. How can you be sure that those around you will follow the right example? 1 Corinthians 11:1 (Philippians 3:17)

_____

_____

15. What is the basic qualification for proving the will of God in your life? Romans 12:1, 2 (2 Corinthians 4:10)

_____

_____

_____

16. In practical terms of everyday living, how then do you experience what is true? John 7:17 (John 8:31, 32)

_____

_____

_____

17. In short, what must you always do to expect God's direction? Proverbs 3:5, 6 (Psalms 62:5)

_____

_____

18. Why is your life in the will of God so blessed? Exodus 33:14 (Isaiah 43:2; Matthew 28:20)

_____

_____

_____

_____

Make Your Own Application

Romans 8:28 is one of the most comforting promises of the Bible. Think through this verse again, noting the conditions set forth, and then explain why you can accept everything that happens to you as working together for good. Recall some illustration of this promise in your life.

_____
_____
_____
_____
_____
_____
_____
_____
_____
_____
_____
_____
_____

Memorize Romans 8:14; Romans 8:28

Our universe is confessedly one of mystery. Fallen man stalks selfishly and unfettered through the world. Though red-handed and highhanded, he is left to his own liberties. This is man's day. God seems to do nothing—so much so that men doubt whether or not He can. Let us who own His name, however, beware lest we, like the scoffer, charge God with folly. In the midst of mounting world misery and mystery there "runs one golden thread of purpose, not the iron thread of doom." God has gracious ends in view. There are things worse than trouble, worse than pain, worse than death. Sin, to God, is the only unendurable—more intolerable even than hell. Ah yes, God hates hell. If the world's mounting miseries will crowd men to Christ and make hell the emptier, they are better than sin. Such is the wisdom of God in a mystery.

—L. E. MAXWELL

Everything which occurs, with the exception of sin, takes place—and yet without infringing on moral liberty—in the divinely appointed order and arrangement of things, and is an expression, within its own appropriate limits, of the divine will. And consequently, in its relations to ourselves personally and individually, it is precisely that condition of things which is best suited to try and to benefit our own state. On a moment's reflection it will be seen that this important principle raises us at once above all subordinate creatures, and places us in the most intimate connection with God himself.

—THOMAS C. UPHAM

Christ's Cross is the sweetest burden that ever I bear; it is such a burden as wings are to a bird, or sails to a ship, to carry me forward to my harbor.

—SAMUEL RUTHERFORD

There is a time coming in which your glory shall consist in the very thing which now constitutes your pain. Nothing could be more sad to Jacob than the ground on which he was lying, a stone for his pillow! It was the hour of his poverty. It was the season of his night. It was the seeming absence of his God. The Lord was in the place and he knew it not. Awakened from his sleep he found that the day of his trial was the dawn of his triumph! Ask the great ones of the past what has been the spot of their prosperity and they will say, "It was the cold ground on which I was lying." Ask Abraham; he will point you to the sacrifice on Mount Moriah. Ask Joseph; he will direct you to his dungeon. Ask Moses; he will date his fortune from his danger in the Nile. Ask Ruth, she will bid you build her monument in the field of her toil. Ask David; he will tell you that his songs came from the night. Ask Job; he will remind you that God answered him out of the whirlwind. Ask Peter; he will extol his submersion in the sea. Ask John; he will give the path to Patmos. Ask Paul; he will attribute his inspiration to the light which struck him blind. Ask one more——the Son of God! Ask Him whence has come His rule over the world; He will answer, "From the cold ground on which I was lying——the Gethsemane ground——I received my sceptre there."

The hour of thy loneliness will crown thee. The day of thy depression will regale thee. It is thy desert that will break forth into singing. It is the trees of thy silent forest that will clap their hands. The last things will be first, in the sweet by and by. The thorns will be roses. The vales will be hills. The crooks will be straight lines, the ruts will be level. The shadows will be shining. The losses will be promotions. The tears will be tracks of gold. The voice of God to thine evening will be this: "Thy treasure is hid in the ground, where thou wert lying."

——GEORGE MATHESON, a blind preacher

Lesson 15

PREDESTINED

Do you realize that your salvation from beginning to end was mapped out by God before time began? That's right. Before the sun ever rose in the sky or the ocean waves broke upon the shore, God planned your life in Christ "after the counsel of his own will" (Ephesians 1:11), and in that master strategy of divine grace, He predestined you "to be conformed to the image of his Son" (Romans 8:29). Nothing that God does is ever haphazard.

You see, God could plan your life because He has perfect knowledge of all things, including what men do with their freedom to accept or to reject His purpose for their lives. Consequently, He has always known those who would believe the Gospel and persevere unto the end, just as He has known those who would refuse His purpose and thus separate themselves from His grace.

Get it clear, however. No one is predestined to hell. God "will have all men to be saved, and to come unto the knowledge of the truth" (1 Timothy 2:4). To that end He gives enough grace to every man to believe His Word and be saved. But he does not decide for you. It is only your free consent to His sovereign will that assures you of His election unto salvation.

Yet having made that decision, you realize that you are one of the "elect" in Christ (1 Peter 1:2) whom God from the beginning had "chosen" to be saved (2 Thessalonians 2:13). Furthermore, you know that God has preceded your steps all along the way so that nothing is unforeseen in His blueprint of your life. Your life is meant to be only the fulfillment of His design. You do not know all the details in advance, but He knows——He has planned it all from the beginning, and God never makes a mistake. Just let God have His way, for "his way is perfect" (Psalms 18:30).

According as he hath chosen us in him before the foundation of the world, that we should be holy and without blame before him in love.

Ephesians 1:4

And the world passeth away, and the lust thereof: but he that doeth the will of God abideth for ever.

1 John 2:17

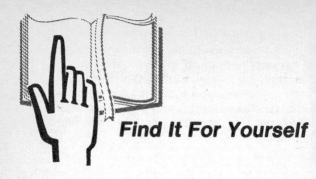

Find It For Yourself

1. In the will of God, when was it decided that Jesus Christ would die for your sins? 1 Peter 1:20 (Revelation 13:8)

_____

2. At the same time, what did God choose you to be by virtue of Christ's work? Ephesians 1:4, 12

_____

3. What were you thus predestined to become in Christ? Romans 8:29 (Ephesians 1:5) —

_____

4. God willed it in the beginning, but what did you have to do in order to realize your promise in Christ? 2 Thessalonians 2:13 (John 1:12; 3:16; 5:24; 12:26, 46)

_____

5. How could God look so far ahead and know that you would believe the gospel and be saved? Acts 15:18 (John 6:64)

_____

6. Since God has always known all things, including your response of faith to His Word, what is your privi-

leged state in His mind? 1 Peter 1:2 (Romans 8:33)

---

7. But you have done nothing to deserve this honor. Upon what basis then does your election in Christ stand? 2 Timothy 1:9 (Romans 9:11; 11:5; Ephesians 1:6)

---

8. Grace means unearned love. Christ accepted justice and gave you mercy. But why would God show you such favor? 1 John 4:8, 10 (Romans 5:8)

---

9. Since God's nature is one of love, how many people does He want to save? 2 Peter 3:9 (1 Timothy 2:4)

---

10. If God wants everyone to be saved, why are some people lost? John 3:18, 36 (John 8:24)

---

11. What is the reason for God's wrath upon the unbeliever in Christ? John 3:19 (Romans 1:18; Ephesians 5:6)

---

12. If disobedience to truth, expressed finally by the rejection of Christ, is the occasion for God's awful judgment upon those who are lost, what characterizes those who are saved by faith in Christ? John 14:21; 15:10 (1 John 2:5)

---

13. As obedient children of God, how should you live in keeping with your calling? 1 Peter 1:14, 15 (1 Thessalonians 4:7)

_____

14. In demonstration of His holiness, state in twenty words how you should act as the elect of God? Colossians 3:12–14 (1 Timothy 6:11, 12)

_____

_____

_____

_____

15. What must you do to make your calling and election sure? 2 Peter 1:10 (Revelation 17:14)

_____

16. Here then is a paradox. In the sense that you must obey the Word of God, who is responsible to work out your salvation? Philippians 2:12 (2 Timothy 4:7)

_____

17. But in the sense that you are totally dependent upon the grace of God for salvation, even your ability to believe and obey, who does all the work? Philippians 2:13 (Ephesians 1:11)

_____

18. The sovereign will of God thus is the ultimate reality with which you must reckon. It is perfect. You can resist it, but you cannot change it. Yet in submitting to God, what wonderful assurance do you have no matter what happens? 1 John 2:17

_____

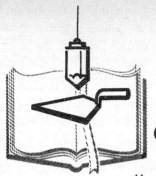

Make Your Own Application

Have you ever wondered why God would ever want to save you, since all along He knew how utterly undeserving of His love you were? In this connection, read 1 Corinthians 1:26–31, and then write your reaction to the knowledge that His salvation included you.

_____

_____

_____

_____

_____

_____

_____

_____

_____

_____

_____

Memorize Ephesians 1:4; 1 John 2:17

In the heat of the crucible, we can know that the Refiner is never far away. The crucible and the gold are His——the fierceness of the fires shall be as nothing in that day when His purified, believing people begin to radiate His praise.

——GEOFFREY BULL

Paul did not take pleasure in infirmities. He tells us that he was anxious to get rid of the infirmity that clouded his life. But when he saw that God supplied the grace he began to love the supply better than freedom from infirmity. He saw that it was better to have darkness with stars brought out by it, than all sunshine and no stars; that the cold winds of winter are as necessary for the world's development as the cheerful warmth of spring and summer. . . . When a man learns that God's strength is perfected through his infirmity, necessities, persecutions, and distresses, he will by and by begin to welcome them as an angel sent from heaven to minister to him.

——A. C. DIXON

The continuation of the justice of the faithful is nothing but the continuation of the infusion of grace and not through one single grace which lives forever. It is this which teaches us perfectly our perpetual dependence on the mercy of God, since if he interrupts its flow ever so little, drought will necessarily set in. In view of this necessity, it is easy to see that we must continually make new efforts to acquire this continued renewal of spirit. For we can preserve the old grace only by our acquiring a new grace, otherwise we will lose that which we think we retain, like those, who, wishing to shut in the light, merely shut in darkness. Thus we must unceasingly watch over the purification of our inner being.

——BLAISE PASCAL

How firm a foundation, ye saints of the Lord,
Is laid for your faith in His excellent word!
What more can He say than to you He hath said,
You, who unto Jesus for refuge have fled?

In every condition, in sickness, in health,
In poverty's vale, or abounding in wealth,
At home, and abroad, on the land, on the sea,
As thy days may demand, shall thy strength ever
    be.

Fear not, I am with thee, O! be not dismayed,
I, I am thy God, and will still give thee aid;
I'll strengthen thee, help thee, and cause thee to
    stand,
Upheld by My righteous, omnipotent hand.

When through fiery trials thy pathway shall lie,
My grace all-sufficient shall be thy supply,
The flame shall not hurt thee; I only design
Thy dross to consume, and thy gold to refine.

E'en down to old age, all My people shall prove
My sovereign, eternal, unchangeable love;
And when hoary hairs shall their temples adorn,
Like lambs they shall still in my bosom be borne.

The soul that on Jesus hath leaned for repose,
I will not, I will not desert to His foes;
That soul, though all hell should endeavor to shake,
I'll never, no never, no never forsake.

——GEORGE KEITH

Young McCall of the Livingstone Congo Mission, when struck down in the midst of his work, said, as his last words, "Lord, I gave myself to Thee, body, mind, and soul. I consecrated my whole life and being to thy service, and now, if it please Thee to take myself, instead of the work which I would do for Thee, what is that to me. Thy will be done."

Lesson 16

ETERNALLY SECURE

Do you understand that your life in Christ is always secure? There is surely no question of this fact in the Bible, although the devil will try to make you doubt it. The life that Christ gives is everlasting (John 5:24). He promises never to leave you nor forsake you (Hebrews 13:5). In Him nothing can ever separate you from the love of God (Romans 8:39). Trials and temptations will come, but in His grasp, no one can pluck you out of His hand (John 10:28, 29). His faithfulness is certain.

Your faith, of course, "is the victory" (1 John 5:4). You are held as you hold. There is no security nor peace to the unbeliever, whether or not that person professes to have once had an experience. You are "kept by the power of God *through faith* unto salvation" (1 Peter 1:5). If you fail to abide in Christ by faith, His life continues, but you no longer participate in it. Be clear at this point. The believer is safe, but only the *believer*.

This saving faith in turn is evidenced in your life by obedience to the revealed will of God. Thus, it is by continuing to follow Christ that you are assured of His life (John 10:27; 8:31, 51). Anyone who turns back is not worthy of the kingdom. God's Word is simply not to be trifled with, and where it is, there must be repentance and appropriation of His forgiving grace through faith.

But though you must exercise diligence "to make your calling and election sure" (2 Peter 1:10), you can be confident of God's help. That which is committed unto Him is in safekeeping (2 Timothy 1:12). When He saves you, Jesus intends to see you through. Just remember that your security is in Christ, not in yourself. Only by His grace can you "do all things" (Philippians 4:13). "Cast not away therefore your confidence, which hath great recompence of reward" (Hebrews 10:35).

For whatsoever is born of God overcometh the world: and this is the victory that overcometh the world, even our faith.

1 John 5:4

My sheep hear my voice, and I know them, and they follow me: and I give unto them eternal life; and they shall never perish, neither shall any man pluck them out of my hand.

John 10:27, 28

Find It For Yourself

1. How long does your life in Christ continue? John 5:24 (1 John 5:11)

   _____

2. Why is your life in Christ eternal? 2 Timothy 1:10 (John 11:25)

   _____

3. How do you continue to partake of His triumphant life while you live? John 11:26 (Colossians 1:23)

   _____

4. How is your saving faith expressed in daily living? John 8:51; 10:27 (1 John 2:6)

   _____

5. If faith does not result in obedience to the Word of God, what is wrong? James 1:22; 2:17 (1 John 2:4)

   _____

6. What can happen if one fails to abide in Christ by faith? John 15:6 (Luke 12:46)

   _____

7. On the other hand, what are you confident of when you are in the hands of Christ? Philippians 1:6 (2 Timothy 1:12)

8. You believe, but what is it that actually keeps you secure? 1 Peter 1:5 (2 Corinthians 13:4)

9. How adequate is the power of God to take care of you in every situation? 2 Corinthians 9:8 (Philippians 4:19)

10. Why can you rest secure in the promises of God? Hebrews 10:23 (2 Thessalonians 3:3)

11. Though you know that God is faithful to His Word, what will come up in your life to try your faith? 1 Peter 1:6, 7 (James 1:2, 3)

12. Who will always be there to sustain you when these temptations arise? 2 Timothy 4:18 (Hebrews 13:5, 6)

13. Why do you know that trials of this world cannot defeat you? John 16:33 (Galatians 1:4)

14. What victorious confidence do you have in Christ no matter what comes? Romans 8:37 (Philippians 4:13)

15. As far as others are concerned, what do you know that they can never do to your experience in Christ? John 10:28, 29 (Romans 8:38, 39)

_____

16. Descriptive of your feeling in the arms of God, what picture comes to mind when you think of John 14:27? (Isaiah 26:3)

_____

_____

_____

17. Knowing that Christ will give you His protection now and His kingdom forever, how should you wait upon the Lord? Hebrews 10:36 (James 1:4)

_____

_____

_____

18. To put it simply, who are those that gain the victory? 1 John 5:4 (Revelation 17:14)

_____

_____

19. Since faith is the key to it all, what can you do to strengthen your faith in God's keeping power? Romans 10:17 (2 Timothy 2:15; 3:15)

_____

_____

_____

Make Your Own Application

The Christian's armor against the evil forces of this world is described very pictorially in Ephesians 6:13–18. Make a free translation of this passage in terms of how you are using this armor to stand against the powers of darkness.

_____
_____
_____
_____
_____
_____
_____
_____
_____
_____
_____
_____
_____

Memorize 1 John 5:4; John 10:27, 28

An old schoolmaster, talking to his class one morning, many years ago, told a story of an early experience he had climbing Mont Blanc in Switzerland.

There were two parties in the little square of the town, making their preparations with the guides. One young Englishman disregarded all the directions of the guides. He loaded himself with things which he positively declared were essential to his plans.

He had a small case of wine and some delicacies for his appetite. He had a camera with which he proposed to take views of himself and his party at different stages of the climb. He had a batch of notebooks in which he intended recording his impressions as he proceeded, which were afterward to be printed for the information, and, he hoped, admiration of the world. A picturesque cap and a gayly colored blanket were also part of his outfit.

The old toughened guides, experienced by many a severe tug and storm in the difficulties ahead, protested earnestly. But it made no impression on the ambitious youth. At last they whispered together, and allowed him to have his own way. And the party started.

Six hours later the second party followed. At the little inn where they spent the first night they found the wine and food delicacies. The guides laughed. "The Englishman has found that he cannot humor his stomach if he would climb Mont Blanc," one of them said grimly. A little farther up they found the notebook and camera; still higher up, the gay robe and fancy cap had been abandoned. And at last they found the young fellow at the summit in leather jacket, exhausted and panting for breath.

He had encountered heavy storms, and reached the top of the famous mountain only at the risk of his life. But he reached it. He had the real stuff in him after all. Yet everything not absolutely essential had to be sacrificed. And his ideas of the meaning of the word "essential" underwent radical changes as he labored up the steep.

Then the old teacher telling the story suddenly leaned over his desk and, looking earnestly at the class, said, "When I was young I planned out my life just as he planned out his climb. Food and clothing and full records of my experiences for the world's information, figured in big. But at forty I cared only for such clothes as kept me warm, and at fifty only for such food as kept me strong. And so steep was the climb up to the top I had set my heart upon that at sixty I cared little for the opinions of people, if only I might reach the top. And when I do reach it I shall not care whether the world has a record of it or not. That record is in safety above."

—a story told by S. D. Gordon

We shall soon be in eternity, and then we shall see what a little matter are all the affairs of the world. . . . Nevertheless we now make ourselves anxious, as though they were great things. When we were little children with what earnestness did we gather bits of tiles, wood, and clay, to build little houses with, and when anyone destroyed them we were greatly distressed at it, and wept; but now we know right well that all that was of little consequence. We shall do the same in heaven one day, when we shall see that our interests in the world were all mere childishness. Let us pursue our childish occupations, since we are children, but let us not catch cold about them; and if anyone throws down our little houses and designs let us not be over-distressed; for when night comes—I mean death—and we must return to our homes, our little houses will all be useless. We must return to our Father's house.

—FRANCIS OF SALES

CROWNED WITH GLORY

Do you see that in Christ already you are a citizen of heaven? It is true. You have title with Him to "all spiritual blessings in heavenly places" (Ephesians 1:3). That is why it is only natural now for your thoughts to turn to "things which are above" (Colossians 3:1). Your possessions are there. Many of your loved ones are there. And someday, by His grace, you expect to be there.

Already Jesus is preparing a place for you in the "Father's house" (John 14:2). It is a city eternal in the heavens, where there is no sorrow, no pain, no loneliness, not even the suggestion of evil. There in the light of His approving smile you will live forever with all the saints of God in the ever-expanding experience of His love and power.

Though you cannot explain everything about it, you know enough to realize that "the sufferings of this present time are not worthy to be compared with the glory which shall be revealed" (Romans 8:18). With this anticipation growing more meaningful as the day approaches, the grave has lost its sting. Death is but the release of your soul from the present bondage of the flesh to go into the immediate presence of your Lord. And someday, when Christ returns at the end of the age, even your old body will be raised incorruptible from the grave and changed into a body like that of His own resurrected body. Crowned then with the appropriate reward for your faithfulness, you will reign with Christ in the glory which was His before the worlds were made.

This is "the hope which is laid up for you in heaven" (Colossians 1:5). Yet it is more than a hope. It is the climactic reality of salvation for which your soul was born, and to which the whole universe is moving, when at last your toil on earth is ended, and clothed with immortality, you enter triumphantly into your Master's joy.

And if children, then heirs; heirs of God, and joint-heirs with Christ; if so be that we suffer with him, that we may be also glorified together.

Romans 8:17

In my Father's house are many mansions: if it were not so, I would have told you. I go to prepare a place for you.

John 14:2

Find It For Yourself

1. What do you become as a child of God possessing eternal life? Romans 8:17 (Titus 3:7)

_____

2. As an equal heir with Christ, what do you receive with Him? Ephesians 1:3, 11 (Colossians 3:24; Matthew 25:34)

_____

_____

3. Though you have the inheritance of Christ now by faith, where is it held in trust? 1 Peter 1:4 (Matthew 6:20)

_____

4. What is this place like that is called heaven? 2 Corinthians 5:1 (John 14:2; Revelation 21:10–27)

_____

_____

5. In striking contrast to this world, what will be absent from the heavenly city of God? Revelation 21:4 (Revelation 7:16)

_____

_____

6. That there will be no disappointment in heaven is certain, but what will you do there to keep busy? Revelation 7:15 (Revelation 22:3)

7. Why will your life of continuing service in heaven be so radiant with joy? John 14:3; 17:24 (Revelation 22:5)

8. Just how clear will your vision of Christ be in heaven? Revelation 22:4 (1 John 3:2)

9. What is death like to a Christian? Philippians 1:21–23 (2 Corinthians 5:4, 8)

10. In the instant of death your soul goes to be with Jesus, but what will ultimately happen to your body which has lain in the grave? Romans 8:11, 23 (2 Corinthians 4:14)

11. When will this resurrection of your body occur? 1 Thessalonians 4:16, 17 (Colossians 3:4)

12. How will your resurrected body differ from the body which you have now? 1 Corinthians 15:44, 53 (2 Corinthians 5:4)

13. What will your new spiritual body look like? Philippians 3:21 (1 John 3:2)

_____

14. In addition to getting a new body like His own, what will take place that concerns your deeds in the old body? 2 Corinthians 5:10 (Matthew 16:27)

_____

15. What do you look forward to receiving at the judgment? 2 Timothy 4:8 (1 Corinthians 4:5)

_____

16. Since the life of heaven is now unseen with the eye, how can you affirm these things to be true? 1 Thessalonians 4:15 (Hebrews 6:17–19)

_____

17. What then does a study of the Scriptures give you for the future? Romans 15:4 (Colossians 1:5)

_____

18. With this hope firmly set before you, how does it affect your life now? Philippians 3:14, 20 (Hebrews 11:8–16)

_____

_____

19. As you continue to press on to the prize of your inheritance in Christ, what about heaven now should fill your soul? Colossians 1:12 (Revelation 19:5–7)

_____

20. Whether you live or die, what is it that makes you rejoice? Romans 14:8

_____

Make Your Own Application

Read slowly the songs of praise heard in heaven as recorded in Revelation 4:10, 11; 5:11–14; 7:9–12; 15:3, 4; 19:1–6. Compose in a few sentences a song that expresses something of the praise of God which you feel in your heart. Paraphrase the heavenly songs if you wish.

_____

_____

_____

_____

_____

_____

_____

_____

_____

_____

_____

Memorize Romans 8:17; John 14:2

Part Three
Deeper In The Holy Spirit

Every time we say, "I believe in the Holy Spirit," we mean that we believe that there is a living God able and willing to enter human personality and change it.

——J. B. PHILLIPS

The fullness of God is in Christ, and Christ lives in men through His Spirit. He is Himself the gift. He brings all the blessings of Grace, and Wisdom, and Power, but He is the Blesser and the Blessing. There is in the soul a very true sense of a divinely real Presence. The Spirit makes the Presence real. This is the crowning mystery and glory of Grace. The Christian religion is not a set of doctrines about Christ, neither is it a rule of life based on the teaching and example of Christ. It is not even an earnest and sincere endeavor to live according to the mind and spirit of Christ. It is Life, and that Life is the Life of Christ. It is a continuation of the Life of the Risen Lord in His Body which is the Church, and in the sanctified believer. "Christ liveth in me" is the essence of the Christian religion as set forth in the New Testament. It is not a system, but a Presence; the Spirit of Christ indwelling the spirit of man.

——SAMUEL CHADWICK

I will meditate and be still, until something of the overwhelming glory of the truth fall upon me, and faith begin to realize it: I am His Temple, and in the secret place He sits upon the throne. . . . I do now tremblingly accept the blessed truth: God the Spirit; the Holy Spirit; Who is God Almighty dwells in me. O my Father, reveal within me what it means, lest I sin against Thee by saying it and not living it.

——ANDREW MURRAY

Come, Holy Ghost, Creator, come,
  Inspire these souls of Thine;
Till every heart which Thou hast made
  Be filled with grace divine.
Thou art the Comforter, the gift
  Of God and fire of love;
The everlasting spring of joy,
  And unction from above.
Enlighten our dark souls, till they
  Thy sacred love embrace;
Assist our minds, by nature frail,
  With Thy celestial grace.
  —Latin of 12th Century (translated by Tate)

Suppose we saw an army sitting down before a granite fort, and they told us that they intended to batter it down. We might ask them, "How?" They point to a cannon ball. Well, but there is no power in that; it is heavy, but not more than half a hundred, or perhaps a hundred weight. If all the men in the army hurled it against the fort, they would make no impression. They say; "No; but look at the cannon." Well, there is no power in that. A child may ride upon it, a bird may perch in its mouth; it is a machine, and nothing more. "But look at the powder." Well, there is no power in that; a child may spill it, a sparrow may peck it. Yet this powerless powder and powerless ball are put into the powerless cannon; one spark of fire enters it; and then, in the twinkling of an eye, that powder is a flash of lightning, and that ball a thunderbolt, which smites as if it had been sent from heaven. So it is with our church machinery at this day: we have all the instruments necessary for pulling down strongholds, and Oh for a baptism of fire!

—WILLIAM ARTHUR

ANOTHER COMFORTER

What makes a Christian so different from anyone else? And even among Christians, why do some seem to have more winsomeness and power than others?

Merely to acknowledge the obvious differences in temperament, intelligence, and ability, as well as physical stamina, is not enough. Nor does pointing out the environmental and hereditary differences adequately answer the question. These are all factors which certainly influence personality, but they in themselves do not account for the basic differences in people.

Ultimately the decisive factor in human personality is not human at all. It is supernatural—the very Life of God released in Christ through the Holy Spirit. It is His power, His holiness, His love that makes your life different.

His work in you might be compared to electricity in a light bulb. There is no light in the glass, nor in the filament within the bulb. The light comes only when these materials receive the electric current for which the bulb was made. Similarly, there is no spiritual life or holiness in your natural state. It is the Spirit's power coming into you from God that makes your life fulfill its intended purpose.

Being a Christian is not just having the righteousness of Christ imputed to you so that by faith you stand justified before God. If this were all there was to it, Christianity would be little more than a bookkeeping job in heaven. But the presence of the Holy Spirit assures you that the Christian life is much more than this. There is an actual impartation to you of the Divine Nature (2 Peter 1:4). You are literally made "a new creature: old things are passed away; behold, all things are become new" (2 Corinthians 5:17).

Think of what this means! The Eternal Spirit; the present Person of the Godhead, equal in glory with the Father and the Son; the very Being of truth and holiness— "dwelleth in you" (1 Corinthians 3:16). You are the "temple" in which He resides (1 Corinthians 6:19). God is in you. All your redeemed powers are at His command. Nothing could be more tragic in your Christian life than for this fact to be unknown or ignored.

God is the Father in administration; God is the Son in revelation; but God is the Spirit in operation, so that wherever the power of God is manifest, you see the work of the Holy Spirit.

In the very beginning of time, it was by the Spirit that God created the worlds and set the stars in space. By the same mighty power, God still upholds that which He has made, and apart from the Spirit, the universe would revert to nothingness.

It was the Spirit Who made man a living soul and breathed into him the life of God. This original life of holiness was lost when the Spirit was withdrawn from man because of sin. Yet, in God's infinite love, the Holy Spirit always has sought to restore man to His fellowship. Every move that man makes back to God today testifies to this unceasing effort. Evangelism is altogether the work of the Holy Spirit.

It was the Spirit Who prepared the way for Christ's coming through the long centuries of the Old Testament. Not everyone felt His power, but those chosen people who did perform some significant service in God's unfolding redemptive purpose were qualified for the task by the Holy Spirit.

Finally, in the fullness of time, as you would expect, it was the Spirit Who planted the seed of God in the womb of the Virgin so that she conceived and brought forth the Holy Child. Thereafter, it was the Spirit Who led Jesus during the days of His incarnate ministry. All that He did in the flesh, He did in cooperation with the Spirit of God. He anointed Him to preach. He empowered Him to cast out demons. He sustained Him in suffering. At last, He enabled Him to offer up Himself to the Father as your sacrifice for sin, and then in death-rending triumph, He raised Him from the grave.

From beginning to end, God's work is done in the power of the Holy Spirit. Yet this power is not some vague, impersonal energy in the universe. The Spirit is a Person in quality like Jesus, and the life He imparts to you by His indwelling is the Christ life.

This was given particular emphasis by Jesus in the last hours before He was taken to be crucified. He knew that His disciples could only carry on His work effectively as they experienced a deeper relationship with Himself through the Spirit. So following the Last Supper, He gathered His faithful ones around Him, and told them that He would send "another Comforter" to take His place when He returned to the Father (John 14:16).

Jesus was not speaking here about an influence or a doctrine; He was speaking of One just like Himself Who would stand by His people—a real Person Who would fill their lives with His own presence and power. Yet there was this difference. Whereas Jesus in the flesh was limited by His earthly body, now this physical barrier would be removed, and His disciples could abide always in His glorious fellowship.

Of course, the Spirit had already been at work in their lives, but in a more wonderful and enduring way, He was now to glorify Christ within them as a living reality. Until Christ had finished His work on earth, this possibility could not be fully realized. But when He returned to take His place at the right hand of the heavenly Throne, then it was that the Spirit of God was released in power upon His expectant church; not for a few years, but for an age; not on a few special individuals, but on all who would receive Him.

For this reason, your privileges today as a Christian are actually greater than those the disciples enjoyed with Jesus while they walked together along the dusty roads of Galilee. For to you, as to them at Pentecost, the Comforter has come. He is here now——Christ is present without any limitations to effect in you what He has already done for you, and of His power, there is no end.

Howbeit when he, the Spirit of truth, is come, he will guide you into all truth: for he shall not speak of himself; but whatsoever he shall hear, that shall he speak: and he will show you things to come.
He shall glorify me: for he shall receive of mine, and shall show it unto you.

John 16:13, 14

And in that day ye shall ask me nothing. Verily, verily, I say unto you, Whatsoever ye shall ask the Father in my name, he will give it you.

John 16:23

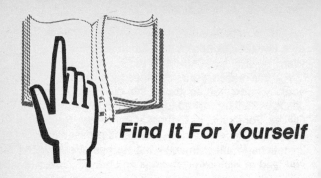

Find It For Yourself

1. When did the Holy Spirit start to work on earth? Genesis 1:2 (Psalms 104:30)

   _____

2. How did the Spirit work through men in the Old Testament? Note the people mentioned in the following verses, and the work which they did in the Spirit:

   (1) Genesis 41:38, 39 _____

   (2) Exodus 31:2–5_____

   (3) Numbers 11:16, 17_____

   (4) Judges 6:34_____

   (5) 1 Samuel 16:13 _____

   (6) What conclusion would you draw from this?

   _____

   _____

3. How does this relate to your view of the Scripture? 1 Peter 1:10, 11; 2 Peter 1:21 (2 Timothy 3:16)

   _____

   _____

4. How was the Spirit instrumental in bringing God directly into the stream of human history? Matthew 1:18, 20 (Luke 1:35)

_____

_____

5. Having given the Son a human body, how did the Spirit continue to work in His incarnate life? Note the particular thing ascribed to the Spirit in:

(1) Luke 4:1 _____

(2) Luke 4:14 _____

(3) Luke 4:18, 19 _____

_____

(4) Matthew 12:28 _____

6. What part did the Spirit play in the atonement finished by Christ on the cross? Hebrews 9:14

_____

7. How did the Spirit work in the resurrection? Romans 8:11

_____

8. How close is the Spirit to every Christian? 1 Corinthians 3:16 (Romans 8:9)

_____

_____

9. By virtue of the Spirit in you, what are some of your privileges through Christ?

   (1) Ephesians 2:18 _____

   (2) Jude 20_____

   (3) John 4:24 _____

   (4) Romans 8:14 _____

10. Various fruits of the Spirit produced in your life are mentioned in Galatians 5:22, 23. Paraphrase each one in your own words.

   _____

   _____

   _____

11. What government exemplifies these spiritual virtues? Romans 14:17

   _____

12. What obligation always rests upon those who live in this Kingdom? Galatians 5:16, 25 (1 John 2:6)

   _____

13. Note some concrete examples of the way the Spirit directed those that walked with Him in the early church. What was the occasion in the following instances:

   (1) Acts 8:29_____

(2) Acts 10:19, 20 _____

(3) Acts 13:2, 4 _____

(4) Acts 15:22, 28 _____

(5) Acts 16:6, 7 _____

14. How does the Spirit react to disobedience? Ephesians 4:30

_____

15. The three chapters in John 14, 15, and 16 record the teaching of Jesus to His disciples on the eve of His death, and as such, comprise our greatest insight into the Person and work of the Holy Spirit. Read through this passage slowly, noting each reference to the Spirit, then answer the following questions:

(1) What is the Name given to the Holy Spirit most often in this passage?

_____

(2) Why would the Holy Spirit be such a Helper to the disciples? What significance does the use of the word "Another" have here? (14:16)

_____

(3) What function does the Spirit have in relation to truth, and your understanding of it? (14:17, 26; 15:26; 16:13)

_____

(4) What is the supreme ministry of the Holy Spirit? (16:14)

_____

(5) Why cannot the unbelieving world receive the Holy Spirit? (14:16, 30; 15:21; 16:3, 8–11)

_____

_____

(6) Why do you think the privilege of prayer is emphasized so much in this passage? (14:13, 14; 15:7, 16; 16:23, 24, 26)

_____

_____

_____

16. In contrast to the way the Spirit moved upon selected individuals for special ministries in the Old Testament, who is included in the potential scope of the promised outpouring of the Holy Spirit in the church age? Joel 2:28 (Acts 2:17)

_____

17. What had to happen in relation to Jesus before the promise of the Comforter could be realized? John 7:39 (Acts 2:33)

_____

_____

_____

Make Your Own Application

Noting John 16:7, tell how Christ is more real to you since the Comforter has come. If you are not sure about it, then write what you think your experience should be as you understand the Scripture. Follow this same course where it applies in other questions throughout the book.

_____

_____

_____

_____

_____

_____

_____

_____

_____

_____

_____

_____

_____

Memorize John 16:13, 14 and John 16:23

The very fact that some of us believe one thing and some another does not do away with the fact that God says, "Be ye filled with the Holy Spirit." I believe this is the greatest need of the church of Jesus Christ today.

Everywhere I go I find that God's people lack something. God's people are hungry for something; God's people are thirsting for something. I find among professing Christians a great need and lack, a feeling of insecurity, and defeat in their Christian lives. . . .

The church today is powerless. We are gathering for our prayer meetings, church services, and Sunday school conventions. Committees meet; Bible classes are conducted; Bible schools are carried on, but we have no power because we do not have the Spirit of God in power and in fulness in our lives. The Bible says, "Be ye filled with the Spirit. . . ."

I want to say something very dangerous. Did you know that it is possible to work for the Lord and live an exemplary life without being filled with the Holy Spirit? It says concerning the Corinthians that they came behind in no gift (1 Corinthians 1:5-7). But Paul called them carnal Christians (1 Corinthians 3:1). This means that I can have the gift of an evangelist. I can get up and preach and still not be filled with the Spirit. I shall preach without power and my preaching will be as sounding brass and tinkling cymbal. You may have the gift of teaching a Sunday school class. You can have the gift without being filled with the Spirit. Because you can get up and talk or teach the Bible does not necessarily mean that you are filled with the Spirit. What an awful thing that is! . . .

I have asked God if there were ever a day when I should stand in the pulpit without knowing the fulness and anointing of the Spirit of God and should not preach with compassion and fire, I want God to take me home to heaven. I don't want to live. I don't ever want to stand in the pulpit and preach without the power of the Holy Spirit.

Some of you may have the gift of administration. You may have the gift of prophecy. You may have any of the other spiritual gifts mentioned in 1 Corinthians 12. You can have all of them and still not be filled with the Spirit! I ask you pastors, I ask myself, I ask you Sunday school teachers, you Christian workers, you church members—are you filled with the Holy Spirit?

—BILLY GRAHAM

It is a very significant thing that in the Epistles, in which we have the maturest Christian experience, we are not told to wait for the Spirit, but to "Walk in the Spirit," and we are not told to receive the Spirit, but to be "filled with the Spirit." We are expressly warned against resisting the Holy Ghost whom we have received, against grieving the Holy Ghost who dwells in us, and against quenching the fire which the Holy Ghost has kindled in our hearts.

I believe it is just here that the root cause of so much of the disappointment and defeat in the Christian life is to be found. We are somewhere, somehow, limiting the Holy One, so that He cannot possess us as He longs to do.

—F. C. GIBSON

Whether here or there, my desire is to know and feel that I am nothing, that I have nothing, and that I can do nothing. For whenever I am empty of myself, then know I of a surety that neither friends nor foes, nor any creature, can hinder me from being "filled with all the fullness of God."

—JOHN WESLEY

Lesson 19

FILLED TO OVERFLOWING

What happened to the disciples at Pentecost, and can it happen again?

That something unusual occurred there in the upper room is obvious. There was a "sound from heaven as of a rushing mighty wind. . . . And there appeared unto them cloven tongues like as of fire . . ." (Acts 2:2, 3). And what was even more startling to the crowds assembled in the city of Jerusalem on that day, the Christians went out on the streets and began to speak so joyfully "the wonderful works of God" in such diverse languages that the people thought they were drunk (Acts 2:5–13). Never had anything like that been seen before.

However, the real power of Pentecost is not to be seen in these great manifestations of the Spirit's outpouring. They attested to God's Presence, but they were only temporary, and like the miraculous signs connected with the advent of the Son of God, need not be repeated.

The enduring miracle of Pentecost is not in the phenomena attending it, but rather in the reality of the experience of Christ which the waiting church received when they "were all filled with the Holy Spirit" (Acts 2:4). This was what made the difference, first in themselves, and then in the world where they lived their witness.

This experience marked a new era in the history of redemption. It was the culminating step in the descent of the divine into the human. Jesus as an external Presence now became the enthroned Sovereign in the hearts of His people. The Gospel became life and power within them, and the church of God went forth determinedly to fulfill the great commission.

The full significance of what this meant becomes increasingly apparent as one studies the Book of Acts. There was a new confidence and boldness in the witness of the disciples. Their hearts burned with the love of God. Attitudes of self-seeking among themselves were gone. They had much to learn, but their hearts were pure. In honor preferring one another, they sought first the Kingdom. Prayer became second nature. The Scriptures opened to them with new meaning and authority. Obedience was joyful. Nothing could defeat them—not the anger of mobs, nor the irritations of daily trials, nor beatings of tyrants, but as rivers borne along with loud rushing sound, they went on their way "with gladness and singleness of heart, praising God" (Acts 2:46, 47).

No wonder the world could not contain them. There was an aroma of heaven upon their lives. Christ was in their midst, and just as He had promised, they were doing the works which He had done (John 14:12). But more than His work, it was His Life filling their hearts with Himself that made the church so different and unconquerable.

It is this reality of being filled with the Spirit that gives to Pentecost an enduring quality. Again and again, mention is made in the Acts that this experience characterized the moving force of the church. In all kinds of situations, in life and in death, individually and collectively, specific reference is made to this spiritual condition undergirding the Christian community.

The words used to describe it are variable. Sometimes the emphasis is upon the act of being filled with the Spirit; at other times it is upon the state of acting in the Spirit. But always the inspired Record underscores the fact, both as an event and as a life.

It accentuates the positive. Without becoming embroiled in theological speculation, the expression simply bears witness to a life situation——a life pervaded by the Spirit of our loving Saviour.

Needless to say, not everyone in the early church was filled with the Spirit. The accounts in the New Testament reflect some problems of strife and pettiness among the believers. However, where these conditions existed, the Spirit-filled reality, variously called, was urged upon the Christians as their privilege and obligation.

This reality still holds good today. The problems which the early church faced were no less real than those which confront you, and God's provision to meet them no less sufficient. Nothing about the enduement of "power from on high" (Luke 24:49) has ever been outmoded. "The promise is unto you, and to your children, and to all that are afar off" (Acts 2:39).

As to that first Pentecost, some have said that the Spirit would have come whether the disciples had tarried or not. Be that as it may, only those who obeyed the Lord, and tarried, received the promise on that day.

So it is with the church today. It is not that a period of time must pass before the heart can be filled. It is simply that the heart must be ready. This is where the issue rests now. The Spirit will surely fill any vessel that is prepared. It remains for you to remove any barrier in His way. Though your vessel may be small, still He can fill you to your capacity. After all, it is not that you get all of Him, but that He gets all of you.

Nor is it a once and for all thing. The command is to be filled with the Spirit continually, moment by moment (Ephesians 5:18). You need to look to God for a fresh outpouring of His Spirit each day. And from time to time, as new problems arise, doubtless you will feel the need for special anointings of the Spirit to meet the demands. So keep open to God; let no selfish rubbish clutter up your life; make Christ Lord in every situation, and you may be sure that the Spirit will continue to fill your soul with the "fulness of God" (Ephesians 3:19).

And be not drunk with wine, wherein is excess; but be filled with the Spirit.

Ephesians 5:18

But ye shall receive power, after the Holy Ghost is come upon you; and ye shall be witnesses unto me both in Jerusalem, and in all Judaea, and in Samaria, and unto the uttermost part of the earth.

Acts 1:8

Find It For Yourself

1. What was the enduement of the Spirit especially to give the disciples? Luke 24:49 (Acts 1:8)

_____

2. How was it symbolized in the figure of baptism? Matthew 3:11 (Acts 1:5)

_____

3. What would the disciples do through the power of the Spirit? Acts 1:8

_____

4. What were the disciples told to do in anticipation of the promise? Acts 1:4 (Luke 24:49)

_____

5. When was the promise realized? Acts 2:1–4, 16

_____

6. In addition to the 120 in the upper room at Pentecost, who else were specifically said to have been filled with the Spirit? Note those involved and the occasion in the following references:

    (1) Acts 4:8 _____

    (2) Acts 4:31_____

(3) Acts 6:3 _____

(4) Acts 6:5 _____

(5) Acts 7:55 _____

(6) Acts 9:17 _____

(7) Acts 11:24 _____

(8) Acts 13:9 _____

(9) Acts 13:52 _____

7. In view of the fact that a number of people are involved in more than one reference to the infilling, what does this suggest to you about the repeated and abiding character of this experience?

_____

_____

8. The reception of the Holy Spirit by the believers at Samaria (Acts 8:5-17), Caesarea (Acts 10:1-48; 11:15-18; 15:7-9), and Ephesus (Acts 19:1-7), while not specifically said to be an infilling of the Spirit, is often associated with it. Review these passages, and summarize in a few words the greatest lesson you learn from these incidents.

_____

_____

_____

9. What did the Holy Spirit do in the hearts of those who welcomed Him? Acts 15:9

_____

10. How did the Holy Spirit enable them to sing amid the trials and frustrations of their day? Acts 13:52 (Acts 2:46, 47)

_____

_____

11. In the face of opposition, what characterized their spoken witness? Acts 4:31; 14:3; 19:8

_____

_____

12. What did they talk about so naturally? Acts 5:42; 8:5; 9:20; 11:20

_____

_____

13. From what you know about the Holy Spirit, why would Christ be the focus of the Christian's witness?

_____

_____

14. An example of such a witness may be seen in Stephen, one of the first lay leaders of the church. Note:

   (1) In addition to being Spirit-filled, why was he selected for a church office? Acts 6:3, 5

   _____

   (2) What made his speech so powerful? Acts 6:10

   _____

(3) What did he accuse the Jews of doing? Acts 7:51

_____

(4) How did the Spirit comfort him as he was being stoned to death? Acts 7:55, 56

_____

(5) What about his last thoughts reflected his deep experience of Christ? Acts 7:60

_____

15. How did the Holy Spirit make the fellowship of the Christians together beautiful? Acts 2:44–47; 4:32–34

_____

_____

16. What disciplines of the holy life did the church practice together? Acts 2:42; 4:24–31; 12:12; 13:2, 3; 17:11

_____

_____

17. What demonstration of God's power frequently attended the witness of the church? Acts 2:43; 5:12; 6:8

_____

18. Whether there were physical miracles or not, what generally followed the Spirit-filled witness of the church? Acts 2:37, 47; 5:14; 6:7

_____

_____

19. As you have observed in reading the Acts, there was
    a great diversity of gifts and offices within the church.
    In this connection, read Romans 12:4–8, 1 Corinth-
    ians 12:4–31, and Ephesians 4:11–15, and note:

    (1) Using the analogy of a body, why are there differ-
        ent gifts, and what purpose do they serve in the
        church?

    _____

    _____

    _____

    (2) Who determines which gift or gifts will be given
        and why? (1 Corinthians 12:11)

    _____

    _____

20. What is the supreme result of the effective exercise
    of spiritual gifts? Ephesians 5:16 (1 Corinthians 13)

    _____

    _____

21. Irrespective of any particular gift which God may be
    pleased to give you, what is His continuing com-
    mand? Ephesians 5:18

    _____

    _____

22. Immediately following this command, why do you
    think the Christians are told to praise God and to be
    subject one to another in the daily relationships of
    life, particularly within the home? Ephesians
    5:19–6:9

    _____

    _____

Make Your Own Application

State several ways in which you believe your family feels the effect of the Spirit's infilling in your life.

_____
_____
_____
_____
_____
_____
_____
_____
_____
_____
_____
_____
_____
_____

Memorize Ephesians 5:18 and Acts 1:8

Lord, I believe a rest remains
    To all Thy people known,
A rest where pure enjoyment reigns,
    And Thou art loved alone:

A rest where all our soul's desire
    Is fixed on things above;
Where fear and sin and grief expire,
    Cast out by perfect love.

O that I now the rest might know,
    Believe and enter in!
Now, Saviour, now the power bestow,
    And let me cease from sin.

Remove this hardness from my heart,
    This unbelief remove:
To me the rest of faith impart,
    The Sabbath of Thy Love.

Come, Father, Son, and Holy Ghost,
    And seal me Thine abode!
Let all I am in Thee be lost;
    Let all be lost in God.

—CHARLES WESLEY

This is the true mark of perfection in Christian love, namely, an entire coincidence of our own wills with the will of God; a full and hearty substitution of the divine mind in the place of our own minds; the rejection of the natural principle of life, which is love terminating in self, and the adoption of the heavenly principle of life, which is love terminating and fulfilled in God; in other words, the expulsion of self from the heart, and the enthronement of God there as its everlasting sovereign.

—THOMAS C. UPHAM

Christian perfection does not imply (as some seem to have imagined) an exemption either from ignorance, or mistake, or infirmities, or temptations. Indeed, it is only another term for holiness. The essential part . . . is giving the heart wholly to God. Your present business is not to reason whether you should call your experience thus or thus, but to go straight to Him that loves you, with all your wants, how great or how many soever they are. Then all things are ready; help, when you ask, is given. You have only to receive it by simple faith. Nevertheless you will still be encompassed with numberless infirmities; for you live in a house of clay, and therefore this corruptible body will more or less press down the soul, yet not so as to prevent your rejoicing evermore and having a witness that your heart is all His. You may claim this: it is yours; for Christ is yours. Believe and feel Him near.

—JOHN WESLEY

Christian perfection is not that rigorous, tedious, cramping thing that many imagine. It demands only an entire surrender of everything to God from the depths of the soul, and the moment this takes place whatever is done for him becomes easy. They who are God's without reserve are in every state content; for they will only what he wills, and desire to do for him whatever he desires them to do; they strip themselves of everything, and in this nakedness find all things restored a hundredfold. Peace of conscience, liberty of spirit, the sweet abandonment of themselves and theirs into the hand of God, the joy of perceiving the light always increasing in their hearts, and finally the freedom of their souls from the bondage of the fears and desires of this world—these things constitute that return of happiness which the true children of God receive a hundredfold in the midst of their crosses, while they remain faithful.

—FRANÇOIS FÉNELON

Lesson 20

THE PROBLEM OF SELF

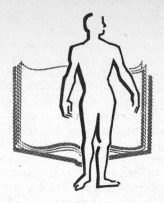

What is the obstruction that prevents the Spirit from filling many Christians?

Certainly God does not want to withhold any good thing from His children. If there is a deficiency in this respect, then, it must be due to the unwillingness of the believer to let God have His way.

This is the problem. All resistance to the will of God must be emptied out of you before the Spirit can fill you.

Sometimes this resistance may be difficult to identify, but it is known in the Bible as "carnality" or "the mind of the flesh" which is "enmity against God" (Romans 8:7). Actually this principle of evil is basically self-centeredness. Its symptoms may take many different forms, such as envy, pride, strife, bitterness, anger, bigotry, revengefulness, jealousy, touchiness, stinginess, pouting, fretting, or some other expression of inward hostility toward God. Wherever this condition is permitted to exist, the flow of the Spirit is clogged, and there is frustration and lack of power in your life.

Of course, if you are unaware of your selfish nature, as may be true of a young Christian living in the enthusiasm of a newfound joy, it may not bother your sense of peace and confidence in the Lord. This may explain why most Christians fail to see the need to do something about it until some bitter experiences have brought it to light.

When the first symptoms begin to come to your attention, probably you have no idea what the root of the matter is. All you know is that something is wrong, and like any good Christian, you confess your failure to God, promising to do better in the future. But as other evidences appear, more and more you become aware that in you "dwelleth no good thing" (Romans 7:18), and perhaps you are led almost to the point of despair, like Paul, when he cried out, "Who shall deliver me from the body of this death?" (Romans 7:24)

Then it is that this carnal disposition has to be faced for what it is. How you are able to deal with the problem, though, hinges on the way that you distinguish it from your essential human nature.

If, as many persons believe, it is so interwoven with your personality that it cannot be distinguished from humanity itself, then all you can do is tolerate it the rest of your life, or, at best, keep it under control. In this case, full relief can be expected only at death when at last your soul is released from your body, or as others claim, only after the fires of purgatory have purified the soul.

However, if you distinguish between your selfish attitude and the essential qualities of your human nature, you are in a position to deal decisively with the problem now. For humanity, like physical matter, is not evil in itself. It has become an instrument of sin, but basically the problem is not with your body, it is with your will——the stubborn, unyielded, independent self unwilling to let God have complete control over your life. For this reason, from this point of view, carnality as a perversion of the will can continue only by your lack of its perception or by your consent. That is why it does not need to be repressed, but crucified.

On the other hand, no matter how dead you are to your carnal self, your human nature remains very much alive. If you fail to accept this fact and fail to interpret your present circumstances accordingly, your whole confidence in what God has done for you can be easily shaken.

In Christian experience your human qualities are not destroyed any more than your self-consciousness is destroyed. You are still a free man. As a free moral personality, you must constantly struggle against all the powers of darkness in this evil world. Temptation will always be real to you, and if you do not continue to yield yourself fully to the Spirit's control, the "old man" can rise again to defeat you.

What complicates the situation is that you must contend with the human limitations inherent in your body and mind. Regrettable as it is, you still have to live with ignorance, even though you try to improve your condition every way possible. Moreover, your physical body, despite all that you can do, is still going to get tired and sick. Then there are hereditary weaknesses which you have to accept. Sometimes, too, scars of the old life before you were converted can hinder your witness, notwithstanding God's forgiveness. Perhaps, also, there are some maladjustments in your behavior growing out of repressed complexes in childhood of which you are not aware. These, and many other involuntary traits, leave much to be desired in this life. Though you seek to overcome them, and can make progress through the help of God, the fact remains that you will not be delivered from most of these infirmities of the flesh until finally your body is glorified in the world to come.

The crucifixion of your carnal nature does not dehumanize you. It will permit the Spirit of Christ to gain the undisputed ascendancy of your will, but it does not deify your nature. You still have your problems, your sufferings, your sorrows. God can keep you sweet amid your trials; however, you will not be insensitive to annoyances or immune to the feelings of pain. You are still human.

Recognizing this truth, it is imperative that you maintain a strict discipline in your will, always keeping your body in subjection to your higher spiritual being. Indeed, in this sense, you must keep your humanity under control of the

Spirit, repressing any tendency that might divert your allegiance from your Lord.

But you do not have to live with that rebellious spirit of carnality. It is sin, and through the blood of Jesus Christ, you can be cleansed from it by the Holy Spirit.

There is therefore now no condemnation to them which are in Christ Jesus, who walk not after the flesh, but after the Spirit.

For the law of the Spirit of life in Christ Jesus hath made me free from the law of sin and death.

Romans 8:1, 2

But he giveth more grace. Wherefore he saith, God resisteth the proud, but giveth grace unto the humble.

James 4:6

Find It For Yourself

1. What was the spiritual state of the disciples prior to their filling of the Spirit at Pentecost?

    (1) Luke 10:20 _____

    (2) John 15:3 _____

    (3) John 17:12 _____

2. There can be little doubt that the obedient disciples of Jesus were saved before Pentecost, but still what unwholesome attitudes characterized their lives? Note the following: (It might be interesting to compare these traits with your own experience.)

    (1) Luke 9:52–55 _____

    (2) Mark 9:34; 10:37 _____

    (3) Matthew 20:24 _____

    (4) Mark 9:38, 39 _____

    (5) Mark 10:13, 14 _____

    (6) Mark 14:37–41 _____

    (7) John 18:18, 25 _____

3. What did Jesus say that seemed so difficult for Peter to accept? Matthew 16:21-23 (Mark 8:31-33)

_____

_____

Why do you suppose this was the case?

_____

_____

4. What does Paul call this fleshly disposition that is at odds with God's will? Romans 8:7 (1 Corinthians 3:1, 4)

_____

5. How does this carnality, or fleshly nature, manifest itself in relation to spiritual things? Galatians 5:17 (Romans 8:5)

_____

6. Read the account of Paul's own struggle with carnality in Romans 7:7-25, noting especially verse 18.

   (1) What did he come to see about himself in the light of God's law?

   _____

   _____

   (2) Why was there a conflict within him?

   _____

   _____

7. How is the carnal mind reflected in the church at Corinth? 1 Corinthians 3:1–4

_____

_____

8. What are some traits of the old nature which still seemed to trouble some of the saints at Ephesus? Ephesians 4:22–32 (Colossians 3:8–10)

_____

_____

_____

9. How does Paul get at the problem when writing to the Philippians? Philippians 2:3, 4, 14

_____

_____

10. What is the cause for instability in the Christian life according to James? James 1:8; 4:8

_____

_____

11. What attitude does God always resist? James 4:6 (1 Peter 5:5)

_____

12. What experience in the Old Testament illustrates the way people who have been saved by God can fail to enter into a victorious life of faith? Hebrews 3:15–19 (Numbers 14:26–33) Try to picture this in your mind.

_____

13. What finally is the crux of the problem with those who are defeated? Hebrews 3:12; 4:2

_____

14. How completely has God dealt with your sin in the atonement of Christ? Hebrews 9:26 (Colossians 2:14)

_____

15. How completely does God expect you to put away sin in your life? 2 Corinthians 7:1 (Hebrews 12:1)

_____

16. Read Romans 7:25–8:4, comparing several translations, and explain why full yieldedness to the Holy Spirit frees you from the old nature of sin and death.

_____

_____

_____

_____

_____

_____

17. Though free from the power of sin, what still remains to be disciplined in your life? 1 Corinthians 9:27

_____

18. What other problem do you have to deal with? Ephesians 6:11, 12 (1 Peter 5:8, 9)

_____

_____

19. Study 2 Corinthians 10:3–5.

    (1) Why are your weapons against Satan so power-
        ful?

    _____

    (2) What must you do with evil suggestions and
        imaginations when they arise out of your circum-
        stances?

    _____

20. What did Christ learn from His human suffering that is
    an example for you? Hebrews 5:8 (Philippians 2:8)

_____

21. What are some habits in Jesus' life which also teach
    you how to get help in strengthening your human na-
    ture?

    (1) Luke 5:16 _____

    (2) Luke 24:27 _____

    (3) Luke 4:16 _____

22. How can your weaknesses in the body become to
    you a means of spiritual blessing? 2 Corinthians
    12:9, 10

_____

23. Who is present now to help you bear your infirmities
    of the body? Romans 8:26

_____

Make Your Own Application

Write out briefly how you recognized your need for a deeper cleansing of the Holy Spirit in your life.

_____

_____

_____

_____

_____

_____

_____

_____

_____

_____

_____

_____

Memorize Romans 8:1, 2 and James 4:6

I awoke that morning hungering and thirsting just to live this life of fellowship with God, never again to sin. . . . Getting out of bed about six o'clock with that desire, I opened my Bible and, while reading some of the words of Jesus, He gave me such a blessing as I never dreamed a man could have this side of heaven. It was an unutterable revelation. It was a heaven of love that came into my heart. My soul melted like wax before fire. I sobbed and sobbed. I loathed myself that I had ever sinned against Him or doubted Him or lived for myself and not for His glory. Every ambition for self was now gone. The pure flame of love burned it like a blazing fire would burn a moth.

I walked out over Boston Commons before breakfast, weeping for joy and praising God. Oh, how I loved! In that hour I knew Jesus, and I loved Him till it seemed my heart would break with love. I was filled with love for all His creatures. I heard the little sparrows chattering; I loved them. I loved the dogs, I loved the horses, I loved the little urchins on the streets, I loved strangers who hurried past me, I loved the heathen——I loved the whole world.

I have never doubted this experience since. I have sometimes wondered whether I might not have lost it, but I have never doubted the experience any more than I could doubt that I had seen my mother, or looked at the sun. It is a living experience.

In time, God withdrew something of the tremendous emotional feelings. He taught me I had to live by my faith and not by my emotions. He showed me that I must learn to trust Him, to have confidence in His unfailing love and devotion, regardless of how I felt.

——SAMUEL LOGAN BRENGLE

Give me a new, a perfect heart,
  From doubt, and fear, and sorrow free:
The mind which was in Christ impart:
  And let my spirit cleave to thee.

O that I now, from sin released,
  Thy word may to the utmost prove!
Enter into the promised rest,
  The Canaan of thy perfect love.

—CHARLES WESLEY

I tell you, as plain as I can speak, where and when I found this. I found it in the oracles of God, in the Old and New Testament; when I read them with no other view or desire but to save my soul. . . .

I say, again, let this perfection appear in its own shape, and who will fight against it? It must be disguised before it can be opposed.

This we confess (if we are fools therein, yet as fools bear with us) we do expect to love God with all our heart, and our neighbor as ourselves. Yea, we do believe, that He will in this world so "cleanse the thoughts of our hearts, by the inspiration of His Holy Spirit, that we shall perfectly love Him, and worthily magnify His holy Name."

—JOHN WESLEY

Self-will will never be satisfied, though it should have command of all it would; but we are satisfied from the moment we renounce it. Without it one cannot be discontented; with it we cannot be content.

—BLAISE PASCAL

SIN AND PERFECTION

Can the Christian be made perfect in this life?

Sooner or later this question is sure to come up. It raises a very delicate problem, but it needs to be answered. Confusion at this point can cause you to live in defeat through constant condemnation of yourself just as it can lead, on the other extreme, to presumption and arrogance.

Let it be settled in the beginning that God expects His people to be holy. He is "of purer eyes than to behold evil" (Habakkuk 1:13). Holy love is the essence of His nature. Without clean hands and a pure heart it is impossible to be accepted in His sight.

The whole purpose of Christ coming into the world was to make a way for man to be acceptable to God. To that end, He died "to redeem us from all iniquity" (Titus 2:14). "He appeared to put away sin by the sacrifice of himself" (Hebrews 9:26). And by His grace, He saves "to the uttermost all that come unto God by Him" (Hebrews 7:25).

This is no academic matter. The blood of Jesus Christ opens to your believing heart an actual deliverance from sin whereby you are enabled by the Holy Spirit to "serve God without fear in holiness and righteousness . . . all the days of your life" (Luke 1:74, 75).

Any time that you sin, then, it is in violation of your privileges as a Christian. You are free to do so, of course, but you cannot get by with it. Deliberate sin will break the fellowship which you have with God, and your soul will come into condemnation. To live with the sense of Christ's Presence, your conscience must be void of offense.

As to how you understand a clear conscience, much depends upon your interpretation of sin. When sin is considered as any deviation from the absolute holiness of God, whether you are aware of it or not, then, of course, you must acknowledge that you sin unconsciously in "thought, word, and deed every day." To do otherwise would require that your mind has no marks of the depravity in the human race. According to this definition of sin, as far as your present experience of righteousness is concerned, you can think of yourself as being free of sin only in the sense of your standing before God by virtue of your identity in Christ.

On the other hand, when sin is considered as a transgression of the known will of God, it is possible to live in Christ each day with the knowledge that there is nothing between you and your Lord. In this case, a distinction is made between a sin of intent and a sin of ignorance or mistake. A sin of intent is a wrong choice issuing from an unholy motive. A mistake is a wrong choice issuing from a holy motive. This does not make the mistaken action any less short of God's Perfection, nor does it absolve you from the consequences resulting from it in this world, but it does mean that your heart is condemned only for what you willfully do against your God.

As an illustration, suppose that you were given permission to go hunting on a certain property, but as you went out to the farm, not knowing clearly the boundaries, you unknowingly crossed the property line. Actually you would be breaking the law by trespassing on another's land, and you might get arrested for it. Morally, however, you would like to think yourself innocent because you were not clearly aware of the boundaries. You made an honest mistake. But having been informed of your error, suppose you went out the next day, traversing the same trail, crossing the same boundary. Whether or not you got caught, you would be guilty of committing a deliberate transgression of the law. You would sin willfully.

Keeping this distinction in mind, there is no reason why your experience in Christ on this earth should not correspond with your standing in Him. Mistakes which you make because of your human imperfections will cause you much regret, and they must be corrected when the Spirit shows them to you, but errors in judgment cannot condemn your soul when you do not know what they are.

Sin, understood as willful transgression, can exist in you only as you permit it. God wants your full consent to His will, and when you choose His side against your own, you come out against sin. As far as you know your heart, you want to live completely set apart for your Lord.

If you do allow yourself to be overcome with temptation, and give way to sin, your heart is broken when you realize that you have given consent to something displeasing to God. In such an event, your normal recourse is to immediately ask Him to forgive you, and with a new resolve of faith, walk in the light of His holiness. But this gracious provision for restoration of His fellowship does not mean that you must continually sin. Rather, it underscores the need for constant holiness through the cleansing blood of Jesus, and emphasizes that if any sin does mar this abiding experience, then you should turn quickly to God in contrition. Thanks be unto God, you never have to go to bed at night with a guilty conscience.

The term "sinless perfection" probably confuses the issue in the minds of many Christians for in any absolute sense, of course, only God is perfect. The only perfection which you can know is your total response to God's will as you know it in Christ. It is not a perfection in knowledge or in accomplishment; it is a perfection in love as God has given you the ability to love—the perfection of your desire to love God with all your heart, with all your soul, with all your mind, and to love your neighbor as yourself (Matthew 22:37–40). This is finally the summation of all the commandments of God.

Such love is holy because it is of God—His own Nature infused into your heart by the Holy Spirit. All you do is open your life fully to His control so that He can love Himself through you. Yet in this yieldedness, you know that your heart is free—free of anything known to be sin, free of condemnation, free of fear—all is well with your soul.

And thou shalt love the Lord thy God with all thy heart, and with all thy soul, and with all thy mind, and with all thy strength: this is the first commandment. And the second is like, namely this, Thou shalt love thy neighbor as thyself. There is none other commandment greater than these.

Mark 12:30, 31

And we have known and believed the love that God hath to us. God is love; and he that dwelleth in love dwelleth in God, and God in him.

1 John 4:16

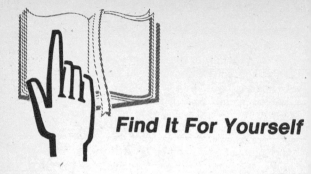

Find It For Yourself

1. What should your attitude always be toward sin? Psalms 97:10 (Proverbs 8:13)

_____

_____

2. Why is this your attitude? Psalms 99:9 (1 Peter 1:16)

_____

3. Who alone can be acceptable in God's sight? Psalms 24:3–5 (Hebrews 12:14)

_____

4. Study 1 Thessalonians 4:7, 8.

   (1) To what has God called you? _____

   _____

   (2) What does resistance to the call mean?

   _____

5. What was God's answer to the sin problem? Matthew 1:21 (Hebrews 7:25)

_____

_____

6. Write out Titus 2:14 in your own words.

_____

_____

_____

_____

7. How long does God expect you to live in holiness on this earth? Luke 1:75

_____

8. In line with this, what did Jesus tell those who received His blessing?

   (1) John 8:11 _____

   (2) John 5:14 _____

9. How did Paul counsel the Christians in regard to living in sin? 1 Corinthians 15:34 (Romans 6:12, 15)

_____

_____

10. Read carefully 1 John 3:1–10, noting especially what is said about sin. Use a modern translation, if possible.

   (1) How is sin defined? (3:4)_____

_____

   (2) Why did Christ appear? (3:5, 8) _____

_____

(3) How are Christians distinguished from others in
    the world? (3:1, 7, 10)

_____

_____

(4) Verses 6, 8, 9, and 10 speak of the contradiction
    of sin in the life of a Christian. The verbs here
    express a habitual action. They do not say that
    a Christian is incapable of committing an act of
    sin, but they do clearly say that a Christian will
    not make a habit of sinning. With this in mind,
    write out in your own words a free translation of
    verse 9.

_____

_____

_____

11. If you do sin, and fellowship with Christ is broken,
    what assurance do you have? 1 John 2:1

_____

_____

12. What danger is there to the man who keeps on sin-
    ning without regard to Christ, continually refusing to
    repent? Hebrews 10:26 (Again the verb in this verse
    expresses a habitual action.)

_____

_____

13. Where does Jesus locate the issue of sin? Mark 7:21–23 (Matthew 5:27, 28)

_____

14. Who alone is qualified to tell you specifically what sin is in your heart? Psalms 139:23, 24 (Jeremiah 17:10)

_____

15. As an example of how the measure of light may vary with Christians, note how the Spirit-filled Peter, like many others, lived for a long time with a wrong assumption.

   (1) What was it? (Acts 10:28)

   _____

   (2) When God corrected his sincere though mistaken view, what did he do about it? (Acts 10:34)

   _____

16. Read the Sermon on the Mount in Matthew 5, 6, and 7, and then list several areas in your life where you feel there might be room for improvement. If you have any explicit idea what you can do about it, jot it down, too.

_____

_____

_____

_____

_____

_____

17. What is the standard for conduct which Jesus lays down for you? Matthew 5:48

_____

_____

18. Compare this with the great commandment of Jesus in Matthew 22:36–40. What strikes you as being at the heart of both, and explain why?

_____

_____

_____

19. What is the bond of perfectness? Colossians 3:14

_____

20. List the things which have no value apart from love as noted by Paul in 1 Corinthians 13:1–3.

_____

_____

_____

21. Where does such love come from? Romans 5:5 (1 John 4:7)

_____

22. Why does perfect love give you confidence and peace? 1 John 4:18

_____

_____

Make Your Own Application

Noting Paul's testimony in Acts 23:1 and 24:16, tell how your conscience backs up your witness of heart purity. Refer also to 1 John 3:21.

_____
_____
_____
_____
_____
_____
_____
_____
_____
_____
_____
_____

Memorize Mark 12:30, 31, and 1 John 4:16

I felt the ingratitude, the danger, the sin of not living nearer to God. I prayed, agonized, fasted, strove, made resolutions, read the Word more diligently, sought more time for meditations——but all without avail. . . . Each day brought its register of sin and failure, of lack of power. To will was indeed "present with me," but to perform I found not.

Then came the question, is there no rescue? Must it be thus to the end——constant conflict, and too often defeat? I felt I was a child of God. His Spirit in my heart would cry, in spite of all, "Abba, Father." But to rise to my privileges as a child, I was utterly powerless.

All the time I felt assured that there was in Christ all I needed, but the practical question was——how to get it out. I strove for faith, but it would not come; I tried to exercise it, but in vain. Seeing more and more the wondrous supply of grace laid up in Jesus, the fulness of our precious Saviour, my guilt and helplessness seemed to increase.

When my agony of soul was at its height, a sentence in a letter from dear McCarthy was used to remove the scales from my eyes, and the Spirit of God revealed to me the truth of our oneness with Jesus as I had never known it before. He wrote: "But how to get faith strengthened? Not by striving after faith, but by resting on the Faithful One."

As I read, I saw it all! "If we believe not, He abideth faithful." I looked to Jesus and saw (and when I saw, oh, how joy flowed!) that He had said, "I will never leave thee."

"Ah, there is rest!" I thought. "I have striven in vain to rest in Him. I'll strive no more."

I saw not only that Jesus will never leave me, but that I am a member of His body, of His flesh, and of His bones. . . . The sweetest part, if one may speak of one part being sweeter than another, is the rest which full identification with Christ brings. I am no longer anxious about anything, as I realize this; for He, I know, is able to carry out His will, and His will is mine. It makes no difference where He places me, or how. That is rather for Him to consider than for me; for in the easiest position He must give His grace, and in the most difficult His grace is sufficient.

Nor should we look upon this experience, these truths, as for the few. They are the birthright of every child of God, and no one can dispense with them without dishonoring our Lord. The only power for deliverance for sin or for true service is Christ.

——HUDSON TAYLOR

When I survey the wondrous Cross
  On which the Prince of Glory died,
My richest gain I count but loss,
  And pour contempt on all my pride.

Forbid it, Lord, that I should boast,
  Save in the death of Christ, my God:
All the vain things that charm me most,
  I sacrifice them to His Blood.

Were the whole realm of nature mine,
  That were a present far too small;
Love so amazing, so divine,
  Demands my life, my soul, my all.

——ISAAC WATTS

Sacrifice is the ecstasy of giving the best we have to the one we love the most.

There have been times . . . when I have been tempted to think He asked too much, more than I could give, when for a few moments, submission or obedience have looked too costly to be possible. Only for a moment or two, thank God, for during those moments I have had an appalling glimpse into that awful existence where He is not known and not obeyed, which is Hell. Then He has brought me back to the glorious truth: Sacrifice.

——HANNAH HURNARD

Lesson 22

CONDITIONS TO MEET

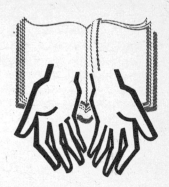

How does one become Spirit-filled? What is the secret of constantly abiding in Christ?

To say that it is perfect love underscores the ethical quality of the condition, but from a practical point of view, love is expressed by obedience, which is the evidence of faith.

God gives the Holy Spirit "to them that obey Him" (Acts 5:32). Your soul is purified "in obeying the truth through the Spirit unto unfeigned love of the brethren" (1 Peter 1:22). The blood of Jesus Christ continues to cleanse from all sin as you "walk in the light, as he is in the light" (1 John 1:7). When this fundamental condition for fellowship with Christ is followed, you should be victorious each step of the way to heaven. Full obedience is perfect happiness when you have unquestioned confidence in Him Whom you obey.

But it is a continuous walk. God never leaves your soul idle and without growth in His Perfection. No sooner will you respond to truth in one area of your life than light will be given in some new direction. For this reason, it is inevitable that along the journey you come to see the inner conflict of self-love, and begin to long for that promised rest.

This desire for something better does not go unrewarded. God "satisfies the longing soul" (Psalms 107:9). Those that hunger and thirst after righteousness shall be filled (Matthew 5:6). Mark it down! When you want God's best more than anything else, you will always find it.

Obedience, of course, brings you to confess any sin when it is pointed out by the Spirit. This means simply that you acknowledge that what God says about your condition is true. When you confess sin, you do not try to hide it, ignore it, or explain it away. But with a broken and contrite heart, you admit the specific transgression committed, asking forgiveness of any person or persons concerned directly in the offense, and offering to make appropriate amends.

Usually the closer you get to the root of your problem of carnality, the harder it becomes to face it. But face yourself you must, confessing your deceitful ego to God, and as with anything else known to be contrary to His holiness, asking Him to cleanse you from it.

There must also be a complete yielding of yourself to God. Your commitment to Christ begun at conversion thus takes on a deeper significance when egotism is nailed to the cross. In a way not known before, you reckon yourself "to be dead unto sin" (Romans 6:11) and "crucified with Christ" (Galatians 2:20). Renouncing your right to yourself, as "a living sacrifice" (Romans 12:1), you abandon all that you are to Jesus.

Whatever it might cost is accepted in advance. It is as though you write your name on a blank check and ask God to fill in the amount which He pleases. You have no desire to be freed from His service, regardless of any suffering and hardship it might entail, even if God would take the sweetness of His Presence from you. You count yourself as nothing but clay in the Potter's Hand.

Such consecration is a fundamental law of the abundant life. Except a grain of wheat fall to the earth and die, it can not bring forth fruit (John 12:24). If there is any resistance to this condition, or if you think yourself better than others because of your compliance with it, then you have not yet fathomed the depths of the carnal mind. In the light of God's love for you, and His sacrifice at Calvary, full and unconditional surrender is your only reasonable response.

Yet, it is not anything that you do that gives the victory. Confession and consecration only prepare your heart to receive the grace of God. The victorious life comes when you actually trust yourself into the possession of Him Who gave Himself for you. Giving up all to Him, you quit your striving, and start resting, just as you would leave an offering upon an altar.

In the final analysis, the infilling of the Spirit, like any other benefit of salvation, is a gift of God. You do not have to beg God for it. The Gift is already present. Indeed, He is in you. All you have to do is to believe that He possesses your empty vessel. You know that the Father delights to "give the Holy Spirit to them that ask him" (Luke 11:13), and if you "ask anything according to his will," you know that He will grant your petition (1 John 5:14, 15).

Your sanctification, then, ultimately rests upon your faith in the Word of God (John 17:17)——the faith that God has chosen you in Christ "before the foundation of the world" that you should be "holy and without blame before him in love" (Ephesians 1:4); the faith that Christ "loved the church, and gave himself for it, that He might sanctify and cleanse it" (Ephesians 5:25, 26); the faith that His precious blood appears in the Holy Place to "purge your conscience from dead works to serve the living God" (Hebrews 9:14); the faith that "where sin abounded, grace did much more abound" (Romans 5:20); the faith that God "is able to do exceeding abundantly above all that we ask or think, according to the power that worketh in" you (Ephesians 3:20); the faith that the Spirit and the Bride bid you come and drink freely from the living waters (Revelation 22:17).

These and a thousand other promises in the Book testify that God is for you, and that all the resources of heaven are available for your full salvation. When you take

Him at His Word, not relying on felt impressions or gifts, but believing only that He shall do what He says, then you may confidently rest in His faithfulness, "for he is faithful that promised" (Hebrews 10:23).

After all, it is not who you are, but Who He is that makes the difference. Rejoice in it. "Faithful is he that calleth you, who also will do it" (1 Thessalonians 5:24).

Seeing ye have purified your souls in obeying the truth through the Spirit unto unfeigned love of the brethren, see that ye love one another with a pure heart fervently.

1 Peter 1:22

I am crucified with Christ: nevertheless I live; yet not I, but Christ liveth in me: and the life which I now live in the flesh I live by the faith of the Son of God, who loved me, and gave himself for me.

Galatians 2:20

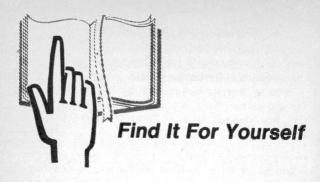

Find It For Yourself

1. What does Jesus promise you in return for your love? John 14:21, 23

   _____

2. How is this abiding fellowship maintained and perfected? 1 John 2:5, 6 (John 15:10)

   _____

3. What does God give to you through obedience? Acts 5:32

   _____

4. What does obedience indicate? Hebrews 11:7, 8 (Genesis 6:9; 17:2)

   _____

5. Note Jesus' teaching in John 8:31, 32.

   (1) Who are the disciples of Jesus?

   _____

   (2) What do you come to know in this relationship?

   _____

    (3) What does this knowledge do?

_____

6. What desire does God honor in satisfying your soul? Psalms 107:9 (Matthew 5:6)

_____

7. What quality of life characterizes those who receive more grace? James 4:6 (1 Peter 5:5)

_____

8. When sin is known in your life, what must you do about it in order to maintain fellowship with your Lord? 1 John 1:9 (Proverbs 28:13)

_____

9. Read the prayer of penitence in Psalm 51, and summarize in a sentence what it teaches you about genuine confession in regard to:

    (1) Honesty_____

_____

    (2) Brokenness _____

_____

    (3) Obedience_____

_____

    (4) Cleansing _____

_____

10. If fellowship is broken with other people, who is responsible for taking the initiative in seeking to restore confidence? Matthew 18:15; 5:24

_____

11. Read the account of the meeting of the disciples in the upper room before Pentecost in Acts 1:12–2:1, and note what you find in regard to:

   (1) Prayer _____

   \ _____

   (2) Study of the Scripture _____

   _____

   (3) Fellowship together _____

   _____

12. What three things did Jesus say that those who follow Him must do? Matthew 16:24 (Luke 9:23)

   (1) _____

   (2) _____

   (3) _____

13. Using an analogy of nature, what did Jesus teach as the fundamental requirement for fruitfulness? John 12:24,25

_____

_____

14. Then how must you reckon yourself in regard to sin?
Romans 6:11 (1 Peter 2:24)

_____

15. How did Paul look upon his own achievements? Philippians 3:7, 8

_____

_____

16. Study carefully Paul's testimony in Galatians 2:20.
Try to put yourself in his place.

(1) How are you associated with Christ? _____

_____

(2) Yet what is the paradox? _____

_____

(3) How then do you live in Christ? _____

_____

17. When you get right down to it, what actually brings
sanctification to you? Acts 26:18; 15:9

_____

18. Using the analogy of a gift laid on the altar, why do
you believe that your dedication is accepted by God,
and therefore made holy? Exodus 29:37; Matthew
23:19

_____

_____

19. Read Hebrews 10:19–23, and note:

(1) Why do you have boldness to ask God for cleansing? (10:19–21)

_____

_____

(2) How must you draw near to God? (10:22)

_____

_____

(3) What about the nature of God gives you confidence? (10:23)

_____

_____

20. Why do you know that God is pleased to give the Spirit when you ask Him? 1 John 5:14, 15; Luke 11:13

_____

_____

_____

_____

21. Sum up Luke 11:13 in terms of your request.

_____

_____

_____

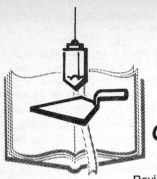

Make Your Own Application

Review your answers in this lesson, and then tell how you have responded to the conditions for the Spirit's fullness.

_____
_____
_____
_____
_____
_____
_____
_____
_____
_____
_____
_____

Memorize 1 Peter 1:22 and Galatians 2:20

At my entrance into religion, I took a resolution to give myself up to God, as the best return I could make for His love, and, for the love of Him, to renounce all besides. . . . Such was my beginning, and yet I must tell you that for the first ten years I suffered much. The apprehension that I was not devoted to God as I wished to be, my past sins always present to my mind, and the great unmerited favors which God did me, were the matter and source of my sufferings. During this time I fell often, and rose presently.

When I thought of nothing but to end my days in these troubles (which did not at all diminish the trust I had in God, and which served only to increase my faith), I found myself changed all at once; and my soul, which till that time was in trouble, felt a profound inward peace, as if she were in the center and place of rest.

Ever since that time I walk before God simply, in faith, with humility and with love, and I apply myself diligently to do nothing and think nothing which may displease Him. . . . As to what passes in me at present, I cannot express it. I have no pain or difficulty about my state, because I have no will but that of God, which I endeavor to accomplish in all things, and to which I am so resigned that I would not take up a straw from the ground against His order, or from any motive than purely that of love to Him. . . . And I make it my business only to persevere in His holy presence, wherein I keep myself by simple attention, and a general fond regard to God, which I may call actual presence of God. . . .

As for set hours of prayer, they are only a continuation of the same exercise. Sometimes I consider myself there as a stone before a Carver, whereof He is to make a statue; presenting myself thus before God, I desire Him to form His perfect image in my soul, and make me entirely like Himself. . . .

The time of business does not differ from the time of

prayer, and in the noise and clatter of my kitchen, while several persons are at the same time calling for different things, I possess God in as great tranquility as if I were upon my knees at the blessed sacrament. . . .

We must, nevertheless, always work at it, because not to advance in the spiritual life is to go back. . . . Let all our employment be to know God; the more one knows Him, the more one desires to know Him. And as knowledge is commonly the measure of love, the deeper and more extensive our knowledge shall be, the greater will be our love.

——BROTHER LAWRENCE

> I want a principle within
>   Of watchful, godly fear,
> A sensibility of sin,
>   A pain to feel it near.
>
> Quick as the apple of an eye,
>   O God, my conscience make!
> Awake my soul when sin is nigh,
>   And keep it still awake.
>
> O may the least omission pain
>   My well-instructed soul,
> And drive me to the Blood again
>   Which makes the wounded whole.

——CHARLES WESLEY

Take care to make yourself daily more pure in heart: this purity consists in weighing everything in the balance of the sanctuary, which is nothing else than the will of God.

Know that it is the virtue of patience that insures us the most perfection; and if we must have it with others we must also have it with ourselves. Those who aspire to the pure love of God have not so much need of patience with others as with themselves.

——FRANCIS OF SALES

CRISIS AND PROCESS IN SANCTIFICATION

When does sanctification begin? Is it a process or an event? Can it be complete in this life?

The issue raised in these questions is often a matter of contention, and it occurs primarily because sanctification is not kept in Scriptural balance.

Basically the word "sanctify" means, in its sacred use, to set apart for God or to make holy, and therefore it takes on the meaning of separation. The noun "saint" is applied to persons who have been sanctified. "Holiness" comes from the same word, and refers to the nature of that which belongs to God.

A problem inevitably arises when sanctification is made to refer almost exclusively to the cleansing of the carnal nature of man following conversion. That sanctification embraces this experience is true, but it has a much wider meaning.

Actually the whole work of the Holy Spirit in conforming the believer to the image of Christ falls within the sphere of sanctification. As such, it begins at conversion when you are "born of the Spirit" (John 3:8). Thus, it can be said that "if any man have not the Spirit of Christ, he is none of his" (Romans 8:9). Every Christian, in this sense, is sanctified, and may be called properly a saint.

However, this is only the beginning. The sanctifying Spirit will never stop trying to bring every area of your life "unto a perfect man, unto the measure of the stature of the fulness of Christ" (Ephesians 4:13). Sanctification thereby becomes a process throughout life by which the obedient child of God progressively is changed into the likeness of Christ, "from glory to glory, even as by the Spirit of the Lord" (2 Corinthians 3:18).

What is sometimes called "entire sanctification," or as Luther translated this compound word in 1 Thessalonians 5:23, sanctification "through and through," is an expression that points to a particular work of the Spirit in the developing process of redemption. It is never intended to suggest that this is where sanctification begins or ends. While it involves a definite confrontation of truth in relation to the self life, nonetheless, it is only a part of the continuing sanctifying process.

Because the nature of this particular point in Christian experience requires the deepest commitment of the will, the decision which it forces often stands out as a monumental crisis. The carnal self does not die easily, and for those who struggle against the claims of God, the final agony of the struggling ego might resemble the last gasps of a puffed-up pillowcase before it goes through an old washing machine wringer. In such cases, when the last yes to the will of God is finally wrung out, it is not unusual for the soul to feel such a release that there is scarcely room to contain the erupting joy. With others there may be no struggle at all, and the crisis of decision may come so gradually, almost without feeling and interwoven with so many other things, that knowledge of its reality may be only the quiet awareness that it has come.

The manner and form will vary in each case, and it is dangerous to try to force it into any prescribed pattern. God made each person different. He suits the blessing to you as He knows best. Whether or not it is accompanied by some dramatic sign or intense emotional feeling at a particular point in time makes the fact of the cleansing and infilling no less real.

It is this definiteness about the fact of the experience itself which prompts some people to speak of it as "a second work of grace.'' The expression is not meant to depreciate the first work, but rather to say that when the Christian comes to see the conflict caused by this selfish nature, and is willing to surrender the problem to God, that the sanctifying grace received at the beginning is also adequate to meet this deeper need.

There will be many other crises in your life growing out of your developing experience of Christ's obedience. Some of these problems will present to you very real spiritual battles, and doubtless will stand out as epochal events in your Christian growth. In facing these decisions, however, you should have the inward strength of a heart already fully committed to the will of God.

Yet, this is a commitment that must be renewed in some way each time a decision of any kind is made, for everything that comes up—in the family, at school, on the job—involves your dedication to Christ. For this reason, it would be better not to think of full consecration primarily as a crisis, but as a life. The life is made up of a constant series of decisions, and how you make each one will determine the blessedness of your experience in following Christ.

As has been intimated several times, full yieldedness to the Spirit does not imply that you are completely mature in Christ. The "second blessing," if it may be called that, merely prepares the way for greater blessings, and growth in the image of Christ is accelerated. Death to self has implications in devotion and service of which you have now no comprehension, but God will be faithful to reveal them to you in the days ahead as you are able to bear them.

So rejoice that there is no foreclosure on progress. No matter what you have experienced thus far, the best is yet to be. As your knowledge of God's purpose grows, and your corresponding obedience of faith enlarges to embrace it, there will be a continual expanding of the Spirit's fulness in your life, even as your days of grace lengthen into the timeless dimensions of eternity.

Your goal is nothing less than the very Perfection of

Jesus Christ. While it remains ever a vision beyond your experience, it is nevertheless a constant incentive to keep pressing on to higher ground, reaching always "toward the mark for the prize of the high calling of God in Christ Jesus" (Philippians 3:14). The closer you get to the heavenly city, the more your soul will long to see His face. Though it does not yet appear what you shall be, you know that when He does appear, you shall be "like him," for you "shall see him as he is" (1 John 3:2).

Whom we preach, warning every man, and teaching every man in all wisdom; that we may present every man perfect in Christ Jesus.

Colossians 1:28

I beseech you therefore, brethren, by the mercies of God, that ye present your bodies a living sacrifice, holy, acceptable unto God, which is your reasonable service.

And be not conformed to this world: but be ye transformed by the renewing of your mind, that ye may prove what is that good, and acceptable, and perfect, will of God.

Romans 12:1, 2

Find It For Yourself

1. How is God's plan of salvation being realized in your life? 2 Thessalonians 2:13 (1 Peter 1:2)

_____

_____

2. Who are the saints? 1 Corinthians 1:2 (Ephesians 1:1)

_____

_____

3. Note in 2 Corinthians 3:18:
   (1) Into Whose image are you being changed?

   _____

   _____

   (2) Who changes you? _____

   (3) When are you changed? _____
   (4) Why do you see Christ now as in a glass?

   _____

4. Write 1 Corinthians 13:12 in your own words. Compare your statement with a modern translation.

_____

_____

5. When will you see Jesus face to face? 1 John 3:2 (Revelation 22:4)

_____

6. How do you expect to be presented to Christ when He comes again? Jude 24 (Revelation 14:5)

_____

7. How does the anticipation of your future life affect your living now? 1 John 3:3 (2 Peter 3:14)

_____

_____

8. Sum up your present situation in the thought of Philippians 2:15.

_____

_____

9. What must you do with your selfish nature when it is recognized? Ephesians 4:22; Romans 6:12, 13, 19

_____

_____

10. The verbs in the above verses indicate a completed action. What does this mean in terms of your commitment?

_____

_____

11. Study 1 Thessalonians 5:23, 24, and note:
    (1) To what extent is sanctification possible?

    _____

    (2) What part of your personality can be preserved
    blameless?

    _____

    _____

    (3) Why can you believe God to do this?

    _____

    _____

    (4) When is this to happen?

    _____

12. Note the presentation called for in Romans 12:1. In
    what sense does this decision bring you to a crisis?

    _____

    _____

    _____

13. There is a definite act of consecration to God, but in
    what sense is there also a continuing decision of
    self-denial? Romans 12:2

    _____

    _____

    _____

14. Renewing your dedication continually, in what do you increase day by day as God gives you more grace?

    (1) Colossians 1:10 _____

    _____

    (2) 1 Thessalonians 3:12 _____

    _____

    (3) 2 Corinthians 9:10 _____

    _____

    (4) Colossians 2:19 _____

15. What is the goal in your Christian growth? Colossians 1:28 (Ephesians 4:15)

16. What is especially a problem with immaturity? Ephesians 4:14

17. Give a definition of a full-grown man according to Ephesians 4:13.

18. Note in Philippians 3:12–15:

    (1) What is Paul's objective? _____

    _____

    (2) What is he doing about it? _____

    _____

    (3) Though Paul says he has not attained perfectly
        his goal, yet in what sense is he perfect?

    _____

    _____

    (4) What about the imperfections in his life?

    _____

    _____

    _____

19. As you press on, like Paul, what must you always
    keep before you? Acts 26:19 (Colossians 3:1, 2)

    _____

    _____

    _____

20. In terms of your character, how do you see yourself
    in heaven? Revelation 19:8; 21:27; 22:4

    _____

    _____

    _____

Make Your Own Application

Read 1 Peter 2:21-24 and Philippians 2:5-8. As you think upon the Example which Christ has given you, what are some things about His perfect life which challenge you to be more like your Master? Make these aspirations into resolutions, and then write out the three which have the greatest priority in your thinking now.

_____

_____

_____

_____

_____

_____

_____

_____

_____

_____

Memorize Romans 12:1, 2 and Colossians 1:28

O my God! Thou alone canst give the peace which we experience in this state. The more the soul offers itself freely and without falling back upon itself, the more it is at liberty. So long as it does not hesitate to lose all and to forget itself, it possesses all.

O Bridegroom of souls, Thou lettest the souls which do not resist Thee experience in this life an advance taste of that felicity. We want nothing and we want all. As it is only the creature which bounds the heart, the heart, never being contracted by the attachments to creatures nor by conversion to self, enters so to speak into Thine immensity. Nothing stops it. It loses itself more and more in Thee. But although its capacity grows infinitely, Thou dost entirely fill it. It is always brimming over.

That, my God, is the true and pure worship in spirit and in truth. Thou seekest such worshippers, but Thou dost scarcely find them. Nearly all seek themselves in Thy gifts, instead of seeking Thee alone by the cross and by deprivation. We want to guide Thee, instead of letting ourselves be guided by Thee. We give ourselves to Thee to become great, but we hold back since we have to let ourselves be made small. We say that we cling to nothing, and we are frightened by the slightest loss. We want to possess Thee, but we do not want to lose ourselves so that we can be possessed by Thee. This is not loving Thee. This is wanting to be loved by Thee. O God! The creature does not realize why Thou hast made it. Teach it and impress in the depths of its heart that the clay should allow itself unresistantly to take all the shapes that the Potter pleases.

——FRANÇOIS FENELON

Fear not to take the irrevocable step, and to say that thou hast once and for all given up self to the death for which it has been crucified in Christ. And trust Jesus *the crucified One to hold self to the cross, and to fill its place in thee with His own blessed resurrection life. . . . In the restfulness and peace and grace of the new life thou shalt have unceasing joy at the wondrous exchange that has been made—the coming out of self to abide in Christ alone.*

—ANDREW MURRAY

O for a heart to praise my God,
    A heart from sin set free,
A heart that always feels Thy Blood
    So freely shed for me!

A heart resigned, submissive, meek,
    My great Redeemer's throne;
Where only Christ is heard to speak,
    Where Jesus reigns alone.

A humble, lowly, contrite heart,
    Believing, true and clean;
Which neither life nor death can part
    From Him that dwells within.

A heart in every thought renewed,
    And full of love divine;
Perfect and right, and pure and good,
    A copy, Lord, of Thine.

Thy nature, gracious Lord, impart,
    Come quickly from above;
Write Thy new name upon my heart,
    Thy new, best name of love.

—CHARLES WESLEY

O that the heaven, and the heaven of heavens, were paper, and the sea ink, and the multitude of mountains pens of brass, and I able to write that paper, within and without, full of the praises of my fairest, my dearest, my loveliest, my sweetest, my matchless, and my most peerless and marvelous well-beloved!

—SAMUEL RUTHERFORD

Lesson 24

THE CHRISTLIKE LIFE

What finally is the expression of your self-emptied, Spirit-filled life? How does the Holy Spirit manifest Himself through you?

This question is not difficult to answer, although it will take eternity to disclose its meaning. For when all is said and done, holiness, being the nature of God, is nothing more nor less than Christlikeness.

It is the Christ life which the Spirit imparts to you. The holiness which you possess is only by virtue of your participation in His nature. Never forget it! Christ is the Holy One, and all you do is let Him live His life through you. Though your capacity to experience His fullness will grow as you mature in grace, at least when you are full of His Spirit, you know that He has all that there is of you at the moment. He is Lord of all.

You love Him supremely, not for what He has given you, but for His own sake. His pleasure is your happiness. Nothing gives you more delight than contemplating His holiness and glory. All you want is more grace to be like Him.

As long as you abide in this disposition, you have perfect peace. Discouragement and anxiety, to the extent that they spring from selfishness, are gone. The conflict of interest is settled. Christ has conquered every enemy, so what have you to fear? And since your reputation and ambition are crucified with Him, what have you to lose? Whatever He chooses for you is accepted joyfully. Whether you live, you live unto the Lord. Whether you die, you die unto the Lord. Whether you live or die, therefore, you are the Lord's (Romans 14:8).

In His abiding, there can be no defeat, for His life is your life; His death is your death; His resurrection is your resurrection; His ascension is your ascension, and His victory is your victory.

In practical ethics, His likeness is most obvious in the transparent sincerity and integrity of your life. There is no sham about it. Nothing phony. Be it at church, in the home, at work or play, you are the same. Men may not appreciate some of your peculiar traits, and probably with good reason, but they should know that your word is true and your character beyond reproach. Nothing so discounts the witness of holiness as inconsistency in ethical behavior.

You must call yourself to strict account. People look to you as the representative of Jesus Christ, as indeed you are, and any blemish on your name is a reflection upon what men will think of His. So protect His honor jealously. "Abstain from all appearance of evil" (1 Thessalonians 5:22). Whenever the Spirit checks you in the least degree, make things right without delay. Mistakes which are made may be observed by others, but let them also see the readiness with which you make apology and earnestly seek through correction to become more like the Master.

The sincerity of your desire to grow in His image is evidenced by your personal devotional life. Carelessness at this point will undermine your highest aspirations. With this in mind, let nothing keep you from communion with God every day through the Word and prayer. Protect your quiet times. Listen to the Spirit of Christ within you. Cultivate the practice of the presence of God in the simple, common, routine chores of living. Here is the index of your spiritual vitality.

Your devotion to God in turn overflows in loving service to those whom He loves and whom Christ died to save. It is in this area where your sanctification finds its deepest relevance to the world. No longer preoccupied with your own frustrations, but motivated by Calvary love, you enter wholeheartedly into the redemptive ministry of your Lord.

In this respect, Jesus sanctified Himself. Not that He needed cleansing or empowering, but that He willingly and continually gave Himself to those He loved that they "might be sanctified through the truth" (John 17:19).

If this dimension of sanctification is neglected, your cleansing from sin and empowering for victorious living would seem to revolve around a selfish purpose, and thereby repudiate the very thing from which you are delivered. The Spirit's work within your heart cannot be self-contained. His sanctification results in making you "a vessel unto honor," not to gratify your desire for personal blessing, but to make you "meet for the master's use, and, prepared unto every good work" (2 Timothy 2:21). As Jesus said, "After that the Holy Spirit is come upon you; and ye shall be witnesses unto me," beginning where you are, and reaching out to the ends of the earth (*see* Acts 1:8).

You dare not be insensitive to the needs of others, for you are a minister of Christ, feeling His compassion, bearing His suffering, "being made conformable unto his death" (Philippians 3:10). Even as He has given you the example, now by His Spirit you must "follow his steps" (1 Peter 2:21).

It will not be easy. There will be many trials. Men will sometimes misunderstand you, and perhaps even revile you. You may see many failures. Those whom you seek to help may not always appreciate your labors. But that is not your concern; it is God's affair. It is your part only to trust and obey. Stay sweet. Keep singing. Return good for evil. Rejoice in your adversities, for in so doing, you show the praise of Him Who has called you out of darkness into light.

Remember that you never stand alone. Your ministry is

shared by the whole body of Christ, the church. As your vision of His mission grows, so also will your sense of need and appreciation for the fellowship of the blood-washed saints of God. Your love for one another actually becomes to the world an illustration of Christ's love. So make it what it should be. Carry one another's burdens. Work together in the bonds of Him Who is Head of the body, that you may be one in Christ, and "that the world may believe" on Him whom the Father has sent (John 17:21).

For whether we live, we live unto the Lord; and whether we die, we die unto the Lord: whether we live therefore, or die, we are the Lord's.

Romans 14:8

And for their sakes I sanctify myself, that they also might be sanctified through the truth.

John 17:19

Find It For Yourself

1. What could the world see in the lives of the unlearned yet Spirit-filled disciples of the early church? Acts 4:13

_____

2. How was Christ normally called by the church? Acts 10:36 (Romans 14:9)

_____

3. What does it mean to say that Christ is Lord of all? Romans 14:8 (2 Corinthians 5:15)

_____

_____

4. Read the prayer of Paul for the church in Ephesians 3:14–21.

   (1) Summarize in a few words what he wants the Christians to know. (3:17–19)

   _____

   _____

   _____

   _____

(2) How is this to be realized? (3:16, 20)

_____

5. Write the formula for a victorious life as found in Romans 13:14.

_____

_____

_____

6. How does this affect the way that you go about your daily work? Colossians 3:23, 24 (2 Corinthians 5:9)

_____

_____

7. Read the 12th chapter of Romans, noting particularly the various duties of the Christian which are spelled out in verses 6–21. Write down a few of the qualities mentioned which you feel need more attention in your life.

_____

_____

_____

_____

_____

8. Why do the things which you suffer for Christ's sake help you? 2 Corinthians 1:5, 6 (Colossians 1:24)

_____

_____

_____

9. What does God's chastening do for you? Hebrews
   12:5–11

_____

_____

_____

10. What is the practical purpose of sanctification? 2
    Timothy 2:21 (1 Peter 1:22)

_____

_____

11. From what you know about the Holy Spirit, why
    would you naturally expect sanctification to have an
    outgoing application? In this connection, look at John
    7:38 and Hebrews 13:12, 13.

_____

_____

12. What is the measure of your love to others? John
    13:34 (1 John 3:16)

_____

_____

13. How do you manifest your love to Christ? John
    21:15–17 (Matthew 25:35–40)

_____

_____

_____

14. Observe in Matthew 9:35–38 the way Jesus minis-
    tered to the people:
    (1) How was He moved when He saw the multi-
        tudes? (9:36)

    _____

(2) Why did He feel sorry for the people? (9:36)

_____

_____

(3) What was the need of the hour? (9:37, 38)

_____

_____

(4) List five people who are potential laborers in the harvest that you will remember in prayer.

_____

_____

_____

_____

15. One of the greatest chapters in the Bible is the high priestly prayer of Jesus in John 17. Read it slowly, then go back and note:

(1) What had Jesus done to glorify the Father? (17:1–5)

_____

_____

(2) For whom does Jesus show the greatest concern in this prayer? Why? (17:6–19)

_____

_____

(3) What specifically does He ask for them? (17:11, 13, 15, 17)

_____

_____

_____

_____

(4) How did Jesus sanctify Himself? (17:19)

_____

_____

   (5) How did He envision the world hearing the Gospel? (17:18, 20)

_____

_____

   (6) How does He think of unity among the redeemed? (17:21–23)

_____

_____

   (7) How many times does a form of the word "give" occur in these 26 verses? What does this suggest to you about the Christian life?

_____

_____

_____

16. In view of your oneness in Christ, what should you do one for another in the church?

   (1) James 5:16 _____

   (2) Hebrews 3:13 _____

   (3) Galatians 6:2 _____

   (4) 1 Thessalonians 4:18 _____

17. How should you feel toward new Christians in the church? 1 Thessalonians 2:7, 8 (Galatians 4:19)

_____

_____

_____

18. As a goal for those you are helping, sum up Paul's objective in Colossians 1:25–29.

_____

_____

_____

19. What is the best way to develop strong Christian leadership in the church? John 13:15; 1 Corinthians 11:1

_____

_____

20. Read the farewell message of Paul to the Ephesian elders in Acts 20:17–36. Note three qualities of his example among them which challenge your commitment.

_____

_____

_____

_____

Make Your Own Application

Looking at your life, make a mental reservation of how many people you have helped to Christ this past year, and how many of these in turn are now bearing fruit. List several definite ways in which you believe that your witness for Christ can be more productive for His glory.

_____

_____

_____

_____

_____

_____

_____

_____

_____

_____

_____

_____

Memorize Romans 14:8 and John 17:19

CONGRATULATIONS!

You deserve commendation for completing these lessons. It was no easy task. Working through the study has demonstrated a beautiful desire and ability to search the Scripture and let the Spirit apply to your heart the Word of truth.

If you would like to continue a directed program on a more advanced level, you might like the devotional Bible study entitled *Written In Blood* (Revell). Tracing bloodstained footprints through the Bible, it helps you see the central theme of God's redemptive revelation, and to appreciate anew that what the blood of Christ accomplished for you, the Spirit of Christ now effects in you.

Of if you would like to pursue an action-orientated study in the personal evangelism of Jesus, get into *They Meet The Master* (Revell). This in-depth approach encourages you to learn how to confront persons with the Gospel.

While growing in your personal devotion, do not forget those around you who may need your strength. Seek them out, and share what God has given to you.

Whatever you do, keep your spiritual life open-ended toward heaven. There is more to be discovered about the life which is yours in Christ. Find it! Believe it! Live in its power and glory! And as you come to know more of the Word written in the Book you will come to know more of the Word living in your heart, Jesus Christ, the Lord of glory.

. . . The best is yet to come

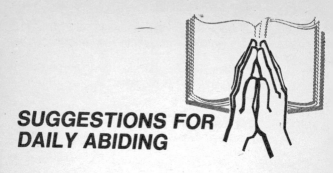

SUGGESTIONS FOR DAILY ABIDING

1. Offer yourself fully to Christ anew each morning, breathing this prayer as you awake: "Lord Jesus, I am Thine, Live Thy life through me today."

2. Thank Him for filling you afresh with His Spirit, and often during the day express to Him your praise for His faithfulness.

3. Take time to wait before Him in earnest prayer and reverent reading of the Scripture.

4. Meditate in your quiet moments upon the fact of His indwelling Presence, realizing that the Spirit of God Himself, the Holy Spirit, occupies your body, mind, and soul.

5. Confess to Him instantly any un-Christlike actions or attitudes which the Spirit reveals to you, and accept His cleansing with thanksgiving.

6. Be honest with all men, speak the truth fearlessly, and desire only God's approval.

7. Obey completely the leading of the Spirit, knowing that He never makes a mistake.

8. Rejoice in your adversities, thanking God that you are counted worthy to enter into His sufferings.

9. Look with Christlike compassion to some person in need of love, and be His minister.

10. Talk about the wonderful works of God, never boasting of your holiness or accomplishments, but be always ready to speak of His.

11. Measure yourself frequently by the Perfection of Christ, and realizing the many failures, omissions, and unimproved opportunities for service which you have unconsciously permitted, resolve to draw closer to Him as He gives you more grace.

12. Commit your way unto the Lord when the day is over, thanking Him for His all-sufficient grace, and close your eyes in the glorious confidence of abiding in Him when you awake.

KEEPING YOUR DAILY QUIET TIME

The most important part of the day, as well as the sweetest, is the time scheduled alone with God. Not that other times are less meaningful, for in God's will every moment is fraught with eternal significance. Jesus would have His followers live continually in an attitude of prayer. But the continuous sense of His Presence is helped immeasurably by a specially appointed period for personal devotion. It brings into focus that communion which should characterize the whole day, and thereby sets the tone of Christian experience.

For this reason, the way you observe a quiet time becomes a good index of spiritual vitality. More than anything else, it shows how much you seek first the Kingdom of God. When nothing is allowed to defeat your practice of God's presence, chances are that you are living victoriously in other areas of privilege. But, if you are careless at this point, probably you have a sense of frustration and failure all along the line.

How is it with you? The following practical suggestions may offer some basis for reflection.

1. Establish Priority

As an exercise in perspective, you might list in the order of importance the things which you want most from life. Hopefully, knowing God and living in fellowship with

Him mean more to you than anything else. But think, too, of your other goals in life.

Now consider how an average day goes. For example, note the time necessary for preservation of your body, including hours for sleep, nourishment and recreation. Add the time for work, family duties, social activity, and personal amusement. Then estimate that part of the day normally given to prayer and spiritual edification. How does it compare with the time you spend watching TV or reading the newspaper? Judging from the overall proportionment of twenty-four hours, how balanced might an unbiased observer regard your desire to grow in body, mind, and spirit?

Taking this kind of inventory may be quite revealing. If the professed goal at the top of your desires falls near the bottom of the day, you need to do something to bring daily life in line with your aspirations.

The issue is not a question of time, but of values. You have time for the things most important to you. If you set a high premium for meeting with God, regardless of other pressing demands, you will take time; if there is no time to take, you must make time. There are no insurmountable barriers to keeping this discipline when you are determined, whatever it takes.

2. Set the Best Time

An audience with the King of Glory deserves that part of the day when your mind is alert. It is presumptuous to drag into His Presence so worn out that you can scarcely think.

Most people find the early morning their best time. Not only is one then refreshed in body, but also some distractions may be avoided that usually come as the day progresses. Incidentally, the secret of getting up early is simply going to bed at a reasonable hour.

Some may prefer a later period in the day, perhaps an off-hour at work, or after the children have gone to school. Others may discover the most convenient time when the daily chores are finished, just before retiring at night. Of course, there is always the option of planning two or three periods at different intervals during the day.

Occasionally you may have difficulty staying mentally awake. In this event, changing postures may help, like kneeling or standing up. You may even try taking a walk. Another way to deal with the problem of alertness is to do some exercises or take a cold shower before starting.

As to the length of the period, fifteen minutes may seem adequate for the beginning Christian, while the pilgrim of many years may feel that hours are not enough. Here you will have to find your own pace. What matters is not the amount of time, but your deep awareness of having met with God. In prayer, quality is always better than quantity. However, occasional seasons of extended meditation, as on a Sunday or holiday, may be valuable as a means of amplifying this principle.

If you miss the scheduled time and cannot arrange another, do not despair. Rather confess the failure, and go on. The next day will afford opportunity to keep the date. But learn from the disappointment, and resolve to be more diligent.

3. Find a Suitable Place

You also need to give attention to the place where you meet God. Obviously, there is an advantage in getting away from loud noises and interruptions.

Look for the place most secluded and least cluttered. When your present location is not suitable, go somewhere else. It might be a room in the house or dormitory, church sanctuary, a park bench, forest, hay loft, any place where you can get alone. More than one person has retreated to the bathroom for some privacy and peace.

If you sit at a desk, it is wise to clear the top of any distracting objects. A clean, orderly appearance naturally stimulates a better mood for relaxed communion. Piled up papers and books tend to remind one of waiting work. To keep from gazing on these things, if necessary, turn your chair facing another direction.

Though not at all essential, you may want to arrange a little worship center, utilizing such things as pictures, biblical symbols, or an altar. Beautiful surroundings out-of-doors also create an effect of wonder and awe, as does appropriate religious music.

4. Come With Expectancy

Anticipation heightens the blessing. Just as a person in love looks forward to seeing his or her beloved, so the prospect of meeting with the Lover of your soul, gazing upon His face, leaves your spirit almost breathless with joy.

Contemplating this experience can be in your mind when waking in the morning and your last thought when your eyes close in sleep at night. The idea fills the day with the fragrance of another world. Heaven seems near. To think that you will soon enter into the Throne Room of the Most High! With this expectancy, you can scarcely wait for the clock to announce the appointed time.

When at last the hour arrives, come before God enthralled with His Sovereignty. Concentrate upon His attributes—His holiness, His love, His justice, His righteousness, His wisdom, His universality, His power.

All these qualities come into focus in Jesus Christ, the Eternal Word made flesh who dwelt among us, the fullness of the Godhead in our likeness. Look into His eyes. See His nail-pierced hands and feet. Walk again around the cross, and ponder the amazing fact: He died for me; He bore my sins away. Then glance beyond Calvary's hill to the open tomb in Joseph's garden, and grasp anew the triumph of His resurrection. The realization is overwhelming. You may not amount to much, but you have a great Savior.

Calling to remembrance a favorite Bible promise may accentuate your confidence. Here is surely one area where memorizing Scripture yields a rich reward. Humming or singing a familiar hymn may serve the same purpose. Whatever the method, you need to get your attention off the things of this world and on to Christ, your Mediator at the right hand of God.

5. Listen to His Voice

Be still, and wait upon the Lord. You may be sure that He is present in His Spirit to lead your obedient heart.

The inspired Word is the vehicle through which He speaks. That is why the Bible is indispensable to two-way conversation. Keep one at hand.

Sometimes a devotional guide may be used for a meditation. There are any number of excellent materials, such as *Daily Light* or Oswald Chambers' *My Utmost for His Highest.* But do not let a book become a substitute for direct exposure to the Book.

The Psalms have long been the greatest source of devotional reading. They reflect the infinite scope of God's nature, as well as the whole spectrum of human need. But you can hear the same still small voice in any portion of the Scripture tuned with your spirit.

You may want to move into some type of Bible study. Answering the questions in this book is an easy way to start in this discipline. As you get more accustomed to thinking through passages, doubtless you will go into more advanced study methods. However, since this involves more expenditure of time, such in-depth study may be reserved for longer and less frequent intervals.

Sincere confrontation with the Word, whatever the approach, invariably opens to you new vistas of truth— promises to claim, exhortations to obey, sins to confess, examples to follow. It is well to have a pencil and paper handy to jot down ideas.

Do not be surprised if on occasion your mind begins to wander, especially in remembering things to do. This is only natural when one stops to think. Simply make a note of the item, then turn your attention back to the business of the Kingdom.

6. Make Your Plans

The counsel of God's Spirit, like a quiet river, flows deep. You are made to see yourself as you are. Debris obscuring your vision is brought to the surface, where it can be removed. Things begin to look a lot clearer. The pieces of the puzzle of your life start fitting together.

Through inner leading of the Spirit, you can make decisions in the light of His calling——what He wants to do in and through your life. Dream together. With His plans before you, you can project realistic goals for the future along with a strategy for accomplishing them.

More immediately, your quiet time permits you to chart a course for the day ahead, committing to God in advance each activity. It also is a time of reflection upon the preceding events, enabling you to learn from past experiences how to fulfill more completely the will of God.

There is never any doubt about His ultimate objective. He intends to conform you to the image of His Son, and someday to present you faultless before His Presence with exceeding joy. Everything that happens to you, good or bad, can be accepted with this assurance. God is for you. His love will never let you go. So rest in His everlasting arms, knowing that what He does is perfect.

7. Talk to the Lord

Prayer issues out of this trust. It is the chatter of a child in love with his Father. You talk with God as you would a friend next to you. He is there listening to every sigh of your heart, and prompting every holy desire. In this manner, the Spirit actually initiates the supplications of your heart.

If you are wondering how to begin, just tell God how much you love Him. Nothing pleases the Father more. Declare His mighty works; make known the glorious honor of His majesty; speak of His unsearchable grace. Words may seem inadequate, but the pulsating attempt of your soul to communicate will be understood.

When you know something is wrong in your life, confess it. Condemnation ruins fellowship. You do not have to explain the situation. God knows all about it. Simply agree with the truth given by the convicting Spirit, turn from sin, and in brokenness, resolve to walk in the way of holiness.

Assured of His forgiveness and power, lay your personal petitions before Him. Do not imagine that anything is too insignificant. He who clothes the lily of the valley surely delights to supply the needs of His own children.

Share with Him, too, the burdens carried for others. The Savior who has borne your sorrows and carried your griefs knows how to succor the heavily laden. He invites you to enter into intercessions for the needy. You may like to make a list of persons to be remembered. Lifting them up to God is your highest ministry.

Prayer closes, much as it begins, in thanksgiving and praise. This is the witness of heaven. Ultimately, it is the only language that will endure.

Through this practice of daily devotion you are being prepared for that perfect communion to come around the Throne of Grace. Whatever form you follow, never lose its thrill. Keep your quiet time fresh and growing. The best is always before you. There is going to be a glorious consummation in the sky.

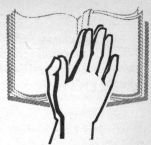

A PRAYER LIST

As a reminder, try making a list of your prayer concerns. You might begin by noting a promise in the Bible which stimulates your faith. This passage can be augmented with others from day to day. With attention centered on God, then you can lift up your own needs. Remember answers to prayer as occasions for thanksgiving. But, most of all, praise God for Himself.

Scripture Promises to Read or Recite from Memory:

_____

_____

_____

_____

_____

_____

_____

_____

_____

Personal Needs:

_____

_____

_____

_____

_____

_____

Others and Their Needs:

_____

_____

_____

_____

_____

Answered Prayers:

_____

_____

_____

_____

_____

_____

_____

SOME TIPS ON BIBLE STUDY

The Christian who learns to study the Bible for himself experiences the perpetual thrill of discovering new riches. But, like finding gold, searching the Scriptures requires skill and much hard work. The treasure usually lies hidden and must be dug up. Only the student who approaches the task with dedication is likely to succeed. With this in mind, you may find the following guidelines helpful.

1. Schedule the time.

Something so important should not be left to chance; it must be planned. A few minutes for serious reflection should be set aside every day, perhaps in connection with your personal devotions. In addition, you may want to arrange a longer period for concentrated study once or twice a week. It might coincide with preparation for a Sunday School lesson or small group assignment. Find what suits your situation and stay with it. Develop the habit of spending unhurried time with your Bible. Regular digestion of God's Word is as essential to your spiritual life as taking food is to your physical growth.

2. Come ready to study.

As basic equipment, you should have a good, well-bound, clear-type Bible. It is well to have several different translations at hand for reference, along with a concordance and a Bible dictionary. Commentaries may prove useful, too, though you must be careful not to rely upon them. If you were to select the aid most helpful, you would probably place a good English dictionary at the top of the list. You will also need a pen or a pencil, and a notebook to jot down your thoughts. By the way, please do not feel that your Bible is too sacred to mark. God wants you to get all you can from His Word, and anything that will help you is pleasing to Him.

3. Follow a definite plan.

In the light of your objective, chart a course. Every journeyman needs a map. To set out on a trip with no prior sense of direction is to invite frustration. As to the best approach, use some form of the inductive method, whereby the Scripture itself is carefully analyzed before making conclusions. Bible study books provide some incentive for getting started, but before long you will need to develop your own program. You may take a book of the Bible and go through it chapter by chapter, verse by verse. Or you might trace a selected theme through the Bible cover to cover. The important thing is that you know where you are going and what you are doing to get there.

4. Open the Bible with prayer.

It is God's Word—infallible, pure, eternal—and should be cherished as a love letter from the Lover of your soul. Hold the message reverently. Knowing that the Spirit is speaking to you through its pages, ask your Teacher to prepare your mind to receive His truth. This implies, on your part, not only a complete confidence in what is written, but also a willingness to do what He says. Every selfish and preconceived notion must be surrendered. When you are fully committed to His will, whatever it may entail, then you can believe God to answer your prayer for understanding. Spiritual illumination comes as an expression of divine grace to the humble and trusting heart.

5. Read to get perspective.

Before you start to interpret a particular verse, go through the chapter, or better still, the whole book to get perspective on it as a unit. A general survey of the context then narrows to exegesis of its parts. Several readings will be helpful in evaluating a passage. One might be rapid and silent; another aloud; and still another rather slow, pausing after each verse to reflect upon what is said. Develop an inquisitive mind, asking yourself questions of the text, always probing the meaning and significance behind the words. Many things may not be clear to you. Simply make a record of the difficulty in the form of a question, and go on. Later, when time permits, you can seek an answer. In this initial reading, just be as honest as you are exact in making observations.

6. Find the writer's purpose.

To understand what the Bible means today, you need to realize first what it meant when written. Put yourself in the writer's place, and visualize the situation through his eyes. Recognize the kind of person he was. How would his previous experience influence the writing? Try to feel his mood, as well as the character of the audience addressed. Observe the location, period in history, ethics of the time, customs of the people, their needs and aspirations. Get before you the reason he wrote, and the main thrust of his message——that pressing conviction dominating the passage. Words and ideas that occur repeatedly may give some indication. Note also lists of items, descriptions, things compared and contrasted, illustrations, cause and effect relationships, warnings, admonitions, and promises. As you come to some judgment about the writer's immediate concern, you are then in a position to relate this to the universal truth for all ages.

7. Understand what the words say.

Inspiration of the Bible is wedded to language, not just thoughts, and each word should be assessed with this in mind. A knowledge of the original tongue, while helpful, is no requirement for understanding if you give proper attention to grammar and sound exegesis. One way to accentuate insight is to check one translation with another. Look up definitions of words which are not clear. As a general rule, words should be understood as bearing their natural meaning unless a good reason appears to indicate otherwise. An important factor is the writer's literary style. Where a poetic, parabolic or apocalyptic form is used, the language may be more figurative than literal. Sentence construction is another vital consideration. Note the subjects and their objects, descriptive adjectives and adverbs, clauses and phrases, and the use of prepositions. Verb tenses are also important, whether the action is completed, in progress or future. And by all means pay attention to the connectives, like "because," "therefore," or "however." These little words are the glue holding ideas together.

8. Compare Scripture with Scripture.

God's Word is a unity, and should be seen as a whole. The Spirit of truth never contradicts Himself. Thus one passage may explain or clarify another. There is no error on earth which may not find apparent support from some isolated text, but no error or practice can stand the light of the complete Revelation. Train yourself to think in terms of the total context, drawing from the full resources of your biblical knowledge. As you learn more about the Bible, your facility to compare verses will increase. As other references come to mind, make a note of them. The marginal notes may also list cross references where the same truth is emphasized. Check them out as there is opportunity. The Scripture has a wonderful way of explaining itself when given a chance.

9. Think through your own position.

Having determined what the Bible actually says, you are now in a position to interpret what the author means. Give your mind plenty of freedom, but be as objective as possible. The principles of study enumerated thus far, if consciously observed, will help you form some personal conclusions. Not everyone will agree with you. Still, you have every right to your own view, recognizing, of course, that you are open to correction if the Spirit may lead into new truth. At this point, it might be well to consult some commentaries to see how others view the subject. While you should not feel bound by these biblical scholars, they may uncover some gems which you overlooked. Do not be surprised, however, if among the "experts" there is still considerable difference of opinion.

10. Summarize the issue.

Reduce the central truth of the passage to its simplest form, whether it be a paragraph, chapter, or book. Anybody can make a truth complicated, but it takes real wisdom to get it down to where a child can understand. One of the best ways to clarify is to paraphrase the passage—putting the content into your own words while preserving the essential truth. That is why, incidentally, you were asked to answer the questions in this book in your own words rather than just repeat the text of Scripture. Drawing up a summary statement is another way to get at it. Or you might make an outline, diagram or chart to show the basic teaching. What counts is that you grasp the main idea. Then you may want to put a handle on it by giving the passage a title for purposes of identification. Where a large passage is involved, pick up a key verse which immediately brings into focus the whole concept. These verses make ideal texts for memory later on.

11. Apply the truth personally.

The Bible is not written to inform, but to change lives. So find out what it means in practice now! Not with reference to everyone in general, but with regard to you in particular. Relate the lesson to your daily experience. You might ask yourself: What does the passage teach about God and His relationship to me? For what am I most grateful? What about my relationships with others? In the home? At work? How are my attitudes affected? Are there actions which I should change? Is some sin pointed out which I need to confess? Do I see an example to follow? A service which I can render to the church or community? What command is there to obey? Do I have a promise to claim by faith? Whatever it is that the Spirit of God lays on your heart, do it! This alone saves Bible study from becoming mere academic pursuit and makes it come alive.

12. Keep Jesus Christ in focus.

Remember throughout that the Scriptures were written to disclose Christ—the fullness of God and the expression of the Word in human personality. Any part of that which is written will point to Him Who is the Way, the Truth, and the Life. To lose sight of this fact is to obscure the whole redemptive purpose of Revelation. Not only is Jesus the Master Key unlocking all the treasures of wisdom, but also He is the Person in Whom your life is being conformed through the Word. Fix your gaze upon Him. Hear what He says. Let His mind guide your thoughts. All that God wants you to know finally begins and ends in His Son whom the Holy Spirit exalts.

Following diligently these basic rules of study, you will always receive illumination from the Scriptures. Some things will remain a mystery. But unresolved problems can be attributed to your lack of information or discernment, rather than to the Bible itself. As you grow in grace and in knowledge, you will continue to see new insights—truths which have been hidden from the ages, things which kings and queens desired to look into, but which God has reserved for His own. Keep digging! You are into God's vein of gold.

SOME TIPS ON MEMORIZING SCRIPTURE

God wants His words to become a part of you, and so deeply that they will swell "in your heart and in your soul" (Deuteronomy 11:18). Only then can you meditate on His laws "day and night" (Psalms 1:2); speak of them while you go about your daily chores (Deuteronomy 6:7); and be ready anytime to give an account of the "hope that is in you" (1 Peter 3:15).

All of this strongly urges you to commit His Word to memory. It is the common sense way to make the Scripture instantly and continuously accessible. Hopefully the Bible verses for memorization in this book have stimulated you to begin laying up this inward treasure. Few spiritual disciplines promise more potential blessing in your personal devotion as well as your witness to others. The following suggestions for an on-going memorization program may be helpful.

1. Declare your purpose.

Intention predisposes retention. The problem in memorization is not a lack of ability, but of desire. You can do anything God asks of you, that is, if you want to. Believe in His adequacy and your determination. By working earnestly, you can make your mind an obedient servant of your heart.

2. Adopt a system.

You need to devise some practical method for keeping your objective in view. It should provide the strategy necessary to keep you on the job, such as minimum goals of new verses to be memorized each week or month, time schedule for observing the discipline, a way of recording memorized verses, and provision for check-up on your progress. Resolutions without a plan seldom materialize. If help is needed in getting a workable scheme, there are a number of programs available in this area from such organizations as Christian Outreach or The Navigators.

3. Select key verses.

Begin with Scriptures most meaningful to your life and ministry. Sometimes you may want to memorize a whole paragraph or chapter coming naturally out of your Bible study and devotion. Note these passages when they catch your attention, perhaps by a marking in your Bible. Before long there will be a backlog of verses which you hope to learn. When there is time, write them down, and bring them into your active memory schedule.

4. Know what the text means.

There is no point in learning something which you do not comprehend. So master the text. This involves an understanding of the words of the memory portion as well as the context out of which the verse is taken. At this point, basic principles of Bible study should be observed. Make the selection live. Visualize the idea. Diagram its parts. Analyze it word by word. Have the verse so clearly in focus that, at its mention, the truth leaps into view.

5. Associate verses with topics.

For usefulness in recall, you can identify each verse with the basic message of the passage. Often some word in the text provides this tag. Thinking of that theme, then, you will immediately remember the specific Scripture. You will eventually accumulate many verses under various categories. If you wish, these general designations can be cross-referenced to indicate relationship.

6. Learn the words perfectly.

Whatever translation you use, memorize the passage exactly as written. Note the punctuation and spelling. It is also important for you to remember where the verse may be found in the Bible. Slipshod quotation destroys the confidence people have in your use of the Word.

7. Repeat the Scripture aloud.

Words uttered audibly become more firmly imbedded in your mind than when recited silently. It is even better when they are said to someone else than to yourself. In saying the verse, also cite the reference. Soon you will have it in your mind. And each time you go over the message, ponder again its meaning and significance.

8. Keep verses with you all the time.

One of the simplest ways to do this is to have your memory verses written on cards so that you can carry them in your pocket or purse. These slips of paper also might be placed in conspicuous places to catch your eye, such as your desk top or dressing mirror. As a matter of policy, too, keep your Bible or Testament within reach. You might need to check something that comes up.

9. Review old verses regularly.

Here is the real secret of memorization. Just as going over the same ground wears a path in your yard, so constant repetition will invariably fix a scriptural portion in your mind. That is why you will probably never forget John 3:16 which has been repeated so many times. You can do this for any verse in the Bible, but you must *review* and *review* and *review*. Begin the process within the first hours after memorization, since you forget more the first day than the next month. Even when you have the verse learned, continue to review it periodically. You might set up some kind of plan whereby you recall verses at weekly, then monthly, intervals.

10. Make the most of spare moments.

Often you can go over the verses without taking any time from your scheduled activity. Why not utilize in this manner the quiet moments you may have waiting for a church service to begin? Consider the time on your hands while riding a bus, taking a walk or at other moments. Alertness here will expand your opportunities for learning and fill your fleeting moments with enduring value.

11. Let someone check on you.

Simply hand your verses to a friend and ask him to see if you say them right. He will be glad to oblige. In fact, it may be a way of drawing you closer together. You may use the occasion to share your love, and also mention how your experience in Christ has been growing richer as you have engraved the Scriptures on your heart.

12. Use the verse all you can.

At this point your labors come to fruition—when the message comes alive in daily experience. The Scriptures stored in your memory provide a well of living water from which you can draw inspiration and direction in prayer. Think on them when making decisions during the day. As opportunity arises, quote the Word in personal conversation. You might even explain what it means, and, in the process, make the idea more unforgettable. Find new and creative ways of doing this according to your own lifestyle.

Through it all, remember that your purpose is not to call attention to yourself, but to lift up Him who is the Truth, the Lord Jesus Christ. Seek to make Him conspicuous, and as you do, you will increasingly know the radiance of His life, and those around you will be drawn to your Saviour.